AT LAST—THE DIET THAT MAKES
OVERWEIGHT TEENAGERS WANT
TO DIET BECAUSE IT PEELS OFF
POUNDS SO FAST . . .

With *The Doctor's Quick Teenage Diet,* Dr. Irwin
Stillman and Samm Sinclair Baker give teenagers
a no-calories-to-count diet of their very own that
takes off pounds and inches the first day. It does
for teenage girls and boys what the famous
Doctor's Quick Weight Loss Diet has done for
millions of adults.

SEE YOUR WEIGHT
GO DOWN FAST

The Doctor's
Quick
Teenage
Diet

by
Irwin Maxwell Stillman, M.D., D-IM
and
Samm Sinclair Baker

PAPERBACK LIBRARY

NEW YORK

PAPERBACK LIBRARY EDITION
First Printing: April, 1972

Library of Congress Catalog Card Number: 72-150670

This Paperback Library Edition is published by arrangement with
David McKay Company, Inc.

Paperback Library is a division of Coronet Communications, Inc.
Its trademark, consisting of the words "Paperback Library"
accompanied by an open book, is registered in the United States
Patent Office. *Coronet Communications, Inc., 315 Park Avenue
South, New York, N.Y. 10010.*

CONTENTS

1. Why You, the Teenager, Can Slim Successfully— at Last 7

2. Your Goal: Ideal Weight for a Slimmer, Healthier Body 25

3. Why Pounds and Inches Vanish Speedily on the Quick Teenage Diet 45

4. The Proved Quick Teenage Diet 53

5. The Super-Quick Teenage Diets 79

6. The 7-Day Quick Teenage Diet 85

7. The Quick Teenage Dividend Diet 97

8. Other Teenage Diets to Drop Pounds Quickly 107

9. Anti-Acne Clear Skin Diet . . . and Other Tips 135

10. Slimming, Trimming Benefits of Activity and Exercise 145

11. Keep-Slim Eating for the Rest of Your Happier Life 163

12. Quick, Easy Recipes for the Quick Teenage Diet 187

13. Talking It Over with the Doctor: Most-Asked Questions and the Answers 215

14. Memo to Parents: How to Help Your Teenager Slim Down and Keep Slim 239

Index 254

*

Dedicated
to our personal teenagers
and teenagers-to-be:

> Anne and Sheryl and Karen and
> Dorothea and Neil and James
> ...and Michael and Caleb

1

Why You, the Teenager, Can Slim Successfully—at Last

This book has one prime purpose: to help you, the teenager, to reduce yourself quickly, healthfully, and successfully—and to help you stay slim for the rest of your more attractive, happier, healthier life. You won't find any "lectures" here, no scolding, no philosophizing or theorizing about manners and morals. My aim is to help you *get that weight off* starting now, and to keep it off.

You can be sure, too, that my instructions include attention to your healthiest growth, to getting enough calcium and other needed elements. You will find effective recommendations to help clear up and control acne and other common teenage skin problems.

Detailed directions for your Quick Teenage Diet start in Chapter 4. I urge you, as a teenager in normal health, to begin the diet at once. Please read the *entire* book as soon as possible, then refer to the various diets you decide to use, and to all the tips and recommendations again and again. Repetition of most important points is necessary, just as usually occurs in repeat visits to a doctor's office, in order to help you most.

Wonderful things can happen for you. Typically, a teenage girl who took off 40 pounds with the Quick Teenage Diet said, "I've discovered that I have a beautiful body! I never realized it before because it was buried under pounds upon pounds of ugly fat."

A young man in his teens who was going to Belgium as an exchange student wrote me: "Tonight I am leaving for a year in Europe, but *30 pounds lighter than before!* Your diet made it possible for me to drop those unwanted 30 pounds in just 3½ weeks. And aside from the great weight loss is a drastic change in my eating habits. I can now turn down nearly anything, from fried chicken to apple pie à la mode, with the greatest of ease. I find that I do diet now, when it's necessary, 'one day at a time.' "

Letters and comments like that from teenagers have furnished some of the greatest thrills I've had in over fifty years of practicing medicine as an internist. Because I know that I've saved many of these young people from the deep sadness of being fat, uncomfortable, and ungainly. In addition, the Quick Teenage Diet has improved their chances considerably for a longer, healthier, more rewarding lifetime, more successful in every way.

I heard an adult remark, "You haven't a chance to reduce teenagers—they stay on the telephone longer than they stay on a diet." I disagree vigorously, and with reason. Unlike those of many grownups, *your habits aren't set yet.* You have a much better chance of succeeding in changing your eating habits and becoming slim. Youth is a time of change, of seeking something better. As an overweight (if you weren't, you wouldn't be reading this), now is your time to lose weight. Being young, you can make the change and reach your goal more easily, more surely.

There's no disputing the fact that habits are created and become fixed over a period of time. Early in life, habits are not so rigid and the pattern is not so firmly set. Therefore it is easier for you, the teenager, to change and succeed in reducing than it is for overweight adults. Other advantages in reducing more readily that teenagers have over adults include increase in height during the growing years, extra metabolic activity, hormonal changes, and other physical and mental differences.

"Why Should Your Methods Succeed In Slimming Me?"

That question is a sensible one and deserves a straight answer. You can count on it—you'll get only frank, clear answers in this book. I have learned through the years that young people want truth, that you can handle your overweight problems better when you understand and have specific instructions to follow.

Now why should I be able to help you reduce successfully, even though you may have failed many times in the past? For many solid reasons: Through my personal practice, and the tens of millions of people of all ages who read my books and magazine articles in many parts of the world, hundreds of thousands of teenagers have been helped to date—perhaps millions. Many thousands of teenagers have slimmed down through my office practice, my work in hospitals and summer camps, and through the mail. I have personally examined, studied, and made recommendations for over 10,000 students in seven huge high schools. In short, many of these teenagers succeeded in reducing, where other methods have failed.

Your optimism and assurance of a better chance to succeed now are thus based on my experience and results with other young people. You will find that I am not hidebound by outmoded theories or by rigid, old-fashioned rules that have failed miserably in most cases. Together we will cooperate to get that unwanted weight off.

In my office, in camps, in talks with large and small groups, I find that teenagers ask the best, the most searching, questions. When I provide the clear answers, as I will do here, they are most apt to benefit wonderfully. My rapid-reducing methods work most effectively for young people, including the large percentage who have failed to slim down by other means time after time. As the pounds and inches vanish, results are speedily seen in improved appearance and health—a clearer, smoother complexion in most cases, a happier viewpoint, and greater enjoyment of living.

In spite of what others may say, I find that teenage overweights are more optimistic in general. You respond more eagerly to my speedy weight-loss methods. You lose weight rapidly, and keep losing it, making it like a game, a sport, to get down to your ideal weight—and to stay there.

Why Many Have Failed in the Past on Other Methods

Unfortunately, most diets are based on hard and un-yielding "balanced eating" rules. Following those common guides, you give up a lot, you stick to the diet instructions, you persevere—and then by the end of the week you've taken off a pound or two at most. You're discouraged, and I certainly can't blame you. Too often you say, "What's the use?" Then you go back to the eating habits that made you overweight in the first place.

There's no denying it, I have observed the sad results too many times—with youngsters especially. If you are slow in losing fat, there's a tendency to give up. But this does not occur on the rapid-result diet. *You can take off 5 to 10 and more pounds per week when you follow my methods exactly.* You look in the mirror each day, you step on the scale and see those numbers going down "miraculously." That visible loss in pounds and inches is precisely the encouragement you need to put aside temptations and to continue to diet.

You don't have to say, "I haven't enough will power"—you can't use that weak alibi any longer as an excuse. The Quick Teenage Diet contains "built-in will power." The wonderful loss in weight that you experience speedily gives you all the will power you need to stay on the diet another day, and another—until you're slim and attractive at your ideal weight.

Another spur to keep dieting is that when you see results you become proud of your success. You appreciate your own self-control. Your slimmer body will be your own accomplishment; you can take the credit for having done it yourself. And that, as you know, is one of the greatest thrills of all. You will go on to learn a new way of eating, a far better way of living. Naturally you gain new confidence, self-assurance, and poise. You appreciate more the happier, slim person who had been hiding inside a fat, unattractive body.

Just Give It One Week

I can assure you that with my speedy reducing methods, you'll lose many pounds and inches in a hurry, at least 5 or more pounds a week—depending on how overweight you are. The heavier you are, the quicker you'll lose. And you'll go on losing week after week . . . surely, healthfully, beautifully.

Just one short week on my Quick Teenage Diet will prove it to you. Certainly, no matter how much you think you like rich, fattening foods, you can do without them for a week. Remember, you're not giving up that much, you're not "starving." You'll be eating good, wholesome tasty foods—lean meats, chicken, seafood, and more. I know from experience that when the mirror and the scale show you inches slimmer and pounds lighter after one short week, that's your biggest incentive to keep on for at least another week and, if needed, another. Realize, too, that you won't be on the diet "forever."

Get it into your head that you only have to diet *one day at a time*. If you start on a Monday, just plan on dieting for that one day. When you arise on Tuesday, figure on that day's dieting. Don't get yourself confused and frustrated by worrying, "How am I ever going to diet through Wednesday, Thursday, Friday, and so on?" Diet one day at a time and you won't be stretching that over-discussed "will power" beyond the breaking point.

Helping you along as you diet is the fact that after a couple of days, the craving for rich, accustomed foods usually diminishes, instead of increasing. Try it with my speedy dieting methods, and see for yourself. Give at least an even break to that slim person struggling to get out of an overweight body. Diet today, and let tomorrow take care of itself. Meanwhile, with each day, your desire for calorie-loaded foods will be less, rather than more.

Another factor in your favor is that from your biology courses and other studies you probably know more about the way the body handles food than many adults who have been away from school for many years. You know that the body is a marvelous mechanism which takes and even manufactures the nutrients it needs from foods. It doesn't need the constant variety of all kinds of foods, the gallons of milk, the "big breakfasts" and other nonsense fed to people year after year.

Your ideas have not yet been "set in concrete." Some people have the mistaken notion that if you don't eat vegetables and fruit and loads of milk plus butter and eggs and so on every day, you'll sicken and die. Any fair-minded scientist can tell you how ridiculous that is. Fortunately, you're young enough not to be blocked by outmoded notions.

You'll read later about the "fake fears" that keep many

overweight adults and too many teenagers stuffing themselves with far more calories than they should have for desirable slimness, good health, and vigor. My program for you is based on scientific facts proved effective in reducing people of all ages, and which contribute to good health.

The way to bad health is to let overweight pounds of fat and flab stay on, right now and as you grow older. The time to start getting that excess, burdensome weight off is now, today. And the way to trim off the unwanted fat is to start dieting with my quick-reducing methods today, and then continue day by day, *one day at a time*. That way you can be sure that there will be a slimmer, trimmer you in your future—and soon. You don't have to wait a month or year from now. You'll be taking off the pounds and inches immediately, pleasantly, safely.

Just Don't Deceive Yourself

According to a philosopher, "The easiest person to deceive is one's self." If you claim that you're following my dieting instructions faithfully, and you still don't lose weight, then chances are that you're fooling yourself. You're doing something wrong such as eating large portions instead of moderate servings, or sneaking in extra foods and special snacks. Otherwise, with my rapid weight-loss methods, your body will be using up more calories than it's taking in (even though you don't count calories).

I questioned a teenage patient after she said that she never strayed from my Quick Teenage Diet and yet wasn't losing weight. She admitted that she had cheated herself. Giggling, she said, "I ate up a big box of cookies —because I didn't want them around to tempt me."

13

Don't Worry About Failing

There's no great tragedy in falling off your diet. The real problem is when you make a big deal out of it and become so disgusted with yourself that you start stuffing in food because you are beset by shame and guilt. Realize instead that you're not the first person, young or old, who fell off a diet. Instead, shrug off the incident, treat it as a lesson you've learned, and start dieting all over again—at once.

Some of my greatest successes, slim and happy teenage boys and girls, have slipped, started again—and finally succeeded beyond their dreams. *Don't ever be discouraged!* The Quick Teenage Diet works—and can certainly work for you. If you fall off the diet, pick yourself up, climb back aboard, and start all over again. A wit put it this way: "Even the woodpecker owes his success to the fact that he uses his head and keeps pecking away until he finishes the job he starts."

Don't blame your excess fat on a faulty metabolism or any other medical problem. ("Metabolism" means primarily how the system produces heat, energy or locomotion, and growth.) If you have any such problem, your doctor will have told you so during your examinations over the years and will do something to help you overcome the imbalance or other difficulty. (As I will advise urgently over and over in this book, have your doctor examine you before you go on *any* diet. Even if you feel perfectly healthy, have no complaints at all, have a checkup by your physician. Discuss with him how you intend to diet before beginning a dieting routine.)

A lower rate of metabolism is generally not a vital factor in overweight, even though it affects the rate at which your food and calories are utilized in your body. If your metabolism is slower than normal, it merely means you need to eat less. In my experience about five teenagers out of a hundred have a moderately low metabolism rate; fewer than one out of a hundred have a

14

very low metabolism rate. That tiny percentage will be given the proper medication by the physician.

So that's another fake excuse out the window. The basic test is whether you tell yourself (and others) the truth about what you eat. Your way to a slim, trim body is through effective dieting, plus plenty of physical activity. Overeating of high-calorie foods is your chief enemy that brings on the bulges—as a comedian put it, "Excess marks the spot."

Your Success Begins with This Single Step

Get started, make up your mind that this is the way that will succeed for you as it has for so many others like you. A magazine showed a teenager standing on tiptoes on a scale and flapping her arms like a bird's wings in order to keep her pounds from showing on the scale (the only benefit she got was the exercise). This is sad, not funny, because even if she could influence the scale, she would still have the unattractive, unhealthy fat on her bulky body. Realize that these quick methods will slim you surely and sensibly—and help keep you trim.

I've heard too many people say incorrectly that teenagers are too impatient for results, that you're overweight because you're "waitless"—that you can't wait long enough for a diet to work. That's not true. Many of my teenage patients have shown more drive and stick-to-it-iveness than adults.

Furthermore, you stop dieting when you reach ideal weight. Then you switch to a variety of foods on Keep-Slim Eating, explained in detail for you later. You don't have to diet "forever"—you just avoid eating an overabundance of calories. If you do put on a few pounds more than you should weigh, you go right back on my Quick Teenage Diet and in a few days are right back at your ideal weight. You have a method of keeping trim and slim to use from now on.

Don't Believe Pessimistic Predictions

One of the "diet specialists" (still a heavy man himself!) states that overweight and obesity amount to "a chronic and permanent disease" which can be controlled but not cured. I differ most strongly with this concept. I have had many extremely overweight patients who have cured their obesity once and for all, maintaining ideal weight year after year. I call overweight and obesity a "storage problem" which is controlled and cured by learning how to remove fat from the storage areas in the body, and preventing fat from accumulating in the future.

Furthermore, my formerly overweight and obese patients in most cases adopt the same eating habits as normally thin people—at teenage and every age. I'm certainly an example—I was obese for years, then took off 55 pounds, and have remained at ideal weight for decades without thinking much about what I eat.

You can cure yourself of overweight for the rest of your life. And you can feel very optimistic about your chance of success.

How Many Teens Are Overweight

Said one overweight teenager, "If we could see ourselves as others see us . . . we'd go on a diet!" That applies to most young people. In my experience, as many as 80 percent of girls from the ages 10 to 18 are overweight. At about 19 years of age, young women especially become more concerned than ever before about their overweight and start reducing. From 18 to 25, about 50 per cent are too heavy. From then on, the percentages grow to about 70 percent of the adult population being overweight.

I find that about 50 percent of boys during the teen years are overweight. When they get into their twenties, many get married, start eating more and being less active, and the number of heavies grows to about 70 percent of the male population. Figures given by others may vary, usually on the low side, but these findings seem more realistic.

For Male and Female Teenagers

Clearly, my quick-reducing methods for teenagers apply to boys and girls alike. Girls are more likely to be heavy, and it's harder for them to lose, as they have less muscle tissue than boys, their metabolism is generally up to 10 percent slower, and their bodies don't utilize their food as efficiently. Also, boys are as a whole more active than girls, using up more calories daily. But that's balanced out since girls usually are more eager to slim down and more likely to follow instructions exactly.

However, the basic rule remains the same: If you consume more calories than you expend, those excess calories become body fat, and the flab piles up on your body—male or female. As you'll learn, you don't count calories—although calories do count. No matter what your sex, the Quick Teenage Diet will slim and trim you swiftly, surely.

How Do Overweight Teens Get That Way?

By the time you reach your teens, you can be sure that you're not burdened with "baby fat," which, they say in error, will come off with time. "Baby fat" is a myth, except as it applies to infants. Any fat that persists after the first couple of years of age, including subcutaneous

17

fat (just beneath the skin), is the same as adult fat. "Baby fat" is present in infants primarily because they sleep a great deal and don't burn up their food as rapidly as when older.

So, if you're in your teens and overweight, don't let anyone fool you with the statement that it's "baby fat," which will vanish magically. Any fat you have is *the real thing*, and it's up to you to do the right thing to get rid of it. You want the truth, I know, and you can take it—because knowing the true facts, you're more likely to take the necessary steps to trim off the flab. You won't wait to "grow out of it"—you'll start reducing effectively now.

Usually, overweight starts with overeating from early childhood. When someone says that "overweight runs in my family," it generally means that the family eating habits are wrong. Extensive studies show that if one parent is overweight, chances are 40 percent that the youngster will be fat. When both parents are overweight, chances are double, about 80 percent, that the child will be heavy. If the family as a whole eats too much, it's more difficult for youngsters to break the habit.

However, all habits can be changed, and the time to start changing overeating habits is right now. The longer you put off taking off weight, chances are the more you'll be putting it on. You'll learn here not to "live to eat" but to eat to live more healthfully, to be slimmer, most attractive and alert. The famous 18th-century French epicure, Brillat-Savarin, said, "Tell me what you eat, and I'll tell you what you are."

What you are is an intelligent human being dedicated to getting the most out of life, to enjoying being healthy, alive, attractive, active in mind and body. You'll come to realize that food is a minor matter, that a person is not just a great big stomach concentrated on stuffing itself. Understanding that, learning how to eat to live most effectively, you can really break the habits that made you overweight in the first place.

It is significant that humans are about the only primates (including monkeys and apes) who eat for the pleasure of eating. The body doesn't need all the food usually eaten by man in order to function most efficiently and healthfully. The general overeating by humans piles fat into the storage centers, and the result is most unhealthy as well as unattractive.

No matter what has happened in the past, it's up to *you* now. You can stop blaming others and take the responsibility yourself. Everybody wants the same thing for you— a better, healthier life free from the physical and mental burdens of excess fat.

Is Activity Important?

While you can never take off enough calories through exercise and activity to take off many excess pounds of fat, keeping active is extremely important for teens, especially, in order to be slim and trim. The vast majority of overweights tend to be sluggish. They usually avoid sports, walking, bicycling, running, any kind of sustained activity and exercise.

To lose weight, to attain the attractive figure you want, I urge you not only to follow my dieting instructions, but also to become more active. Carefully read Chapter 10 on activity and exercise. Then please follow my recommendations starting at once, and from now on.

You don't have to become an "exercise nut." No rigorous calisthenics are necessary or desirable. I highly recommend brisk walking every day. As I've often told my teenage patients: Don't sit if you can stand . . . don't stand if you can walk . . . don't walk if you can run. That's an exaggeration, of course, but it gives you the general idea to *get moving!* I don't advise you to become a muscle-man or a sinewy Amazon—far from it. But I do urge you to *use* the miraculous mechanism which is your body by being active as nature intended.

19

Don't ride in a car if you're going only a short distance —walk briskly instead, enjoy the actions of your arms, your legs, your entire body. Don't take an elevator for a few flights—walk the stairs nimbly. Don't slouch—stand with pride, shoulders back, chin and chest up—you'll look better and trimmer, and you'll feel better instantly.

Lying on a couch or the floor or slouching in an armchair watching TV hour after hour (especially as you munch away) tends to make those pounds pile on. As a teenager put it, "TV blab puts on flab." Enjoy selected programs, but don't let TV or radio or records interfere with or replace being *active*. Avoid napping and sleeping too many hours—get up on your toes instead of being flat on your back too much. You get rid of more calories when you get going physically.

QTD Oxygen Exercise

Very important—learn to breathe deeply. The majority of teenage overweights I've examined were breathing improperly and lacked vital lung capacity. Unless your lung capacity is good, you cannot burn up your food properly and instead convert it to fat that is deposited in the fatty tissues. Oxygen is the draft that burns food most effectively. If you don't breathe deeply and correctly, it's almost like having a low basal metabolism, which tends to promote weight gain and slow up weight loss.

Testing hundreds of overweight teenagers, I found an average vital capacity of the lungs of 55 to 65 percent— that's about half of the normal capacity of 100 to 125 percent. The "half-capacity" is an indication of poor utilization of food. By increasing your lung capacity, which you can do readily, your system burns up your food calories more efficiently and helps you in your slimming success.

Start your increased activity program with this QTD

Oxygen Exercise, a simple breathing exercise to increase lung capacity to the desirable maximum: *Keeping your mouth open slightly, breathe in for a slow count of 5, then expel the air. Repeat this slow breathing five times. Do this exercise at least 5 times a day or more, when you think of it and it's convenient—sitting, standing, lying down*—at least 25 of these "deep breaths" per day.

Doing the QTD Oxygen Exercise five or more times a day is a cinch. It will help to increase your lung capacity and use up calories faster. You'll be on your way with the important activity-exercise part of the reducing program. The rest is given in detail in Chapter 10.

Your Personal Success Is Your Personal Reward

I'm not a parent who promises his child a lollipop as a reward for doing something. From my experience over the years, I have great respect for the teenager. I have learned that practically every overweight teenager wants desperately to be slim, active, attractive. This book contains the instructions that will help you achieve that goal. Your cooperation is the other ingredient needed for a successful result. Your greatest reward is your personal glow of accomplishment when you see your slimmer, trimmer figure in the mirror and hear the admiring comments of others.

The many gratifying letters I've received from enthusiastic, newly slim teenagers prove to me beyond question that you can reach your slimming goal by following my recommendations. Here's a typical statement from a high school senior who used my quick reducing methods: "I was 5′ 9″ and weighed 215 pounds. After going on your diet, in about two months I was down to around 160 pounds—a total of 55 pounds lost . . . I'm presently attending the University, majoring in city planning . . . you really changed my life."

Here's another typical success story from a bright girl who writes: "I've always been fat since I was a baby . . . In kindergarten I was a chubby little cute girl whom everyone liked to pinch. I was chubby in 6th grade when they started weighing us in school in front of friends. I dreaded this because I was about 4' 11" and weighed 124 pounds. In 7th grade I decided to diet. I'd eat no breakfast, no lunch in school, and come home starving. If no one was home I'd eat a box of cookies and then have a little meat and vegetables for dinner, letting everyone think I was really dieting. . .

"I was up to a grand total of 150 pounds. . . Then I went on your diet. In seven days I lost 14 pounds. In school everyone noticed I lost weight and I was really happy, down to 136 pounds. I kept dieting until I weighed 120 pounds and looked like a healthy 14-year-old girl, but I was not able to wear a bikini. We were planning to vacation in December and I was going to have a bikini or burst!

"Well, my goal was 105 pounds, and I stuck with your diet. On December 13th I was 105. Everyone in school told me I looked great. My mother had bought me a shocking pink velour bikini held together by gold links. I have a picture of me in it with a suntan, and I wouldn't get fat again for anything!!!" The "before" snapshot she sent me shows a bulging, moon-faced girl—and written in her handwriting, "What a sight!" In the bikini snapshot the same girl looks like a smiling, beautiful movie starlet.

Your 4-Step Plan

These successes are not exceptional. Here is a simple 4-step plan that will help you reach the same goal. Just determine to succeed, and trust yourself.

1. *Have a medical checkup.* Before you go on any diet, have a checkup by your doctor. He will tell you whether you have a metabolic or other physical disorder, or have

any ailment, which he will then help you correct. He will also consider psychological and mental aspects. My recommendations in this book are for overweight teenagers in normal physical and mental health.

2. *Follow my dieting instructions exactly.* Please read the entire book through (and keep it handy for checking over). The Quick Teenage Diet is most successful when you learn all the why's and how's of real weight loss in addition to the diet itself. Determine to go on the Quick Teenage Diet for at least one week, and the wonderful weight loss will keep you dieting until you're down to desired weight.

3. *Increase your physical activity.* Follow my recommendations for exercise and activity in order to slim and trim your body most quickly and effectively.

4. *When slim, be guided by Keep-Slim Eating.* With the combination of swift reducing and Keep-Slim Eating, you should never again have a depressing overweight problem for the rest of your life. If you gain a few pounds, then return to the Quick Teenage Diet; it will bring you back to your desired weight in a hurry.

This plan is easy to get "under weigh." No matter how many times you may have failed to reduce before, you can succeed now as countless thousands of other overweight teenagers have done, many of them undoubtedly heavier than you. You'll be like the teenager who was asked, "What do you intend to do after you've taken off all your excess flab?" He answered, *"Handsprings!"*

2

*Your Goal: Ideal Weight for a
Slimmer, Healthier Body*

To reach your ideal weight and figure, it helps to
realize this simple point once and for all: There are no
magical pills or potions or miracle foods you can eat that
can make you slim "instantly." Every year something
new crops up, such as the idea that grapefruit is a "miracle," that if you eat grapefruit every day or every meal,
that alone will make the pounds and inches vanish. Forget it! Grapefruit is a fine food, but it has no magical
powers to slim you.

You can't make that fat vanish except by intelligent
dieting. A teenager complained, "Every time I weigh
myself, I'm pounds heavier. I guess there's only one solution—stop weighing myself." There are no shortcuts. My
Quick Teenage Diet will turn you from fat to thin because it cuts your calorie intake drastically though allowing you to eat plentifully. It burns up the fat more
effectively than other diets. And it takes off the pounds
rapidly so that you're encouraged to keep on the diet.

As evidence that it can happen to you, here's proof in
a typical letter from a girl I've never met: "In a short
time my whole life has changed—thanks to your program, I'm 25 pounds lighter and 100 percent happier.
I'm delighted with my new size. My family doctor (who
has known me from early childhood) couldn't believe his
eyes. . . After ascertaining that I hadn't lost 25 pounds
through illness, he decided that my general health had
improved. He agrees wholeheartedly with your method,
doesn't consider it 'too drastic,' and recommends it

highly. You have really done your part to 'help stop inflation.' "

DANGER: STOP, LOOK, AND READ

When you look at yourself and see that you're overweight, the time to stop gaining pounds is right now. The dangers increase if you wait to take off that excess weight. Don't let anyone tell you that fat is healthy—the opposite is true. The people who live longest (proved by surveys among the aged) are those who were *under average weight* most of their lives. Ask any pediatrician or any other doctor about the terrible amount of harm that can be done to the growing youngster, as well as the adult, by excess weight. The list of dangers is almost endless.

Fat imposes a monstrous burden—even if you think you don't feel it now—on the heart, blood vessels, pancreas, liver, joints, muscles, skin—on practically all your organs. Diabetes is common among the heavyweights. Chafing of the skin, lesions, acne and seborrhea (excess oiliness leading to eruptions and other skin difficulties) afflict the overweights more acutely. The dangers of clogging of the arteries increase when fat encases the body.

Medical reports abound with warnings: "Adolescents who have elevated blood pressure and a tendency to gain weight will carry their high blood pressure into adulthood unless treated early." One sure step required is to get your weight down quickly. And it's easier to lose weight now than when you're an adult.

There's a saying, "The lean ones will bury the fat ones." It's true, backed by all the statistics. Overweight is an invitation to illness and trouble. The slim youngsters, as well as adults, are overall the healthiest by far. I don't recommend that you seek to be underweight, but to arrive and stay at ideal weight.

To state that a person should be overloaded with pounds of extra fat in order to be healthier, such as in cases of illness, is just another old wives' tale. When illness strikes an overweight individual, the extra burden of fat on the heart and other organs tends to impede a quick return to health, instead of helping. Realize that each extra ounce of fat contains blood systems and makes demands on the heart, the circulatory and other organs.

In summer camps, I found that overweights were far more often ill and in the clinics than the slim campers, male and female. Not only were the heavies more afflicted with illness and diseases, but they were also constantly having more accidents resulting in cuts, bruises, sprained ankles and knees, and other worse injuries.

Blessed Are the Newly Slim

On the bright side, reduction of weight through my methods produces a new perspective, a new drive, new incentive, and greater determination to be thin and stay slim. I have seen this marvelous result countless times in my practice especially with teenagers. One of the greatest visible changes is usually in improved tone, smoothness, and health of the skin and the hair.

In most cases, with slimming down, skin oiliness and the pustules and scars of acne diminish. Excess perspiration and body odor tend to disappear. Chafing in skin folds, under the arms, between the legs and elsewhere, is relieved. And, as the body thins down, well-being is reflected in a slimmer, more attractive face. It rarely fails as weight goes down, spirits go up. You personally, as an overweight, know too well that the legend of "the happy fat kid" is just a myth. Extra pounds of fat are a drag even on the naturally cheerful individual. Psychologically, the most depressed youngsters are usually the overweights. While being slim is no guarantee of happiness, your chances are better—and you help yourself in every way as you shed the burdens of excess poundage.

27

Do GIRLS Thin Out Naturally
as They Start Menstruating?

A young woman cannot count on the onset of menstruation to thin her out "naturally." This is a period of bodily development, and as the body develops, the surface area increases. The metabolism, although normal, now must take care of a larger frame. If a girl is eating the same as before, she is relatively eating somewhat less than before her spurt of growth.

However, the difference in calorie intake and output is not significant in respect to the overweight girl slimming down without dieting. Furthermore, excessive overweight, if not removed, sometimes interferes with proper menstruation. From every viewpoint, when this stage of development begins, it becomes more vital than ever to remove excess fat from the growing body.

In many cases, a heavy girl tends to be lazier at this stage. She decreases her physical activities and puts on even more weight. It's of prime importance not to pamper oneself with menstruation in general. Take advantage of this evidence of womanhood by becoming more alert, more active, participating in more mental and physical undertakings instead of fewer. The more alive, more active you are, the more likely you are to be slim, trim, and most attractive in body and spirit.

Do BOYS Thin Out Naturally
with Physical Maturity?

You'll be making a big mistake if you're an overweight young man and you're counting on a spurt of growth to thin you "naturally" at puberty (entering the period of sexual capability). The equation still holds—despite that very helpful spurt of growth in height which is likely to occur. If you continue to take in more calories than you use up, overweight will not diminish, but will undoubtedly increase. Even if you tend to slim out drastically, you'll become fat again if you overeat—and don't ever let yourself forget it!

Some boys get heavy because they may think that over-developed muscles and excess fat make them look powerful, strong, and virile. They think that "bigness of body" also indicates robust health, vigor, and stamina. It's not true. Fat does not increase strength; rather it leads to breathlessness, ill health, and many other complications.

The Calorie Equation Counts for Males and Females

Just as surely as 12 inches make a foot, 3,500 calories are roughly the equivalent of a pound of fat. If you eat 1,000 calories more a day than your body uses up each day, then you'll gain an extra pound of fat in about 3½ days—whether you're a boy or girl.

Some boys may think it's "manly" or "cute" to eat a lot. Their parents may contribute to this by almost gloating that "my son (or my daughter's boy friend) is eating us out of house and home." It's stupid to engage in a continuing contest to see how much you can eat or who can eat more—the lowliest ape could probably outeat you.

Overeating involves belly, not brains. Instead of bragging about how much you eat, take pride in controlling yourself and in real accomplishments. It's not "in" socially for a person in any age group to eat too much any more. It's never "in" healthfully to overeat and put on fat and flab.

Recognize the Reasons for Your Overweight

A teenage girl who came to me for treatment was a strong-willed individual, very much overweight, who said point-blank, "I hate being a fatty—but there's nothing anybody can do about it because I have medical problems. . ." I suggested, "Why don't we see. . . ?"

I examined her, but before I could say anything further, she blurted out, "It's no use, Dr. Stillman. I've tried everything to take off weight and I've failed every time, but it's not my fault. Two years ago I took sick when I was away on vacation. The hotel doctor who treated me gave me an injection that must have thrown my system out of whack because I've been gaining weight ever since."

She spoke on and on rapidly, covering a whole catalog of the physical "problems" which she had convinced herself were the cause of her overweight. Finally I was able to interrupt. "There's one thing you haven't mentioned among your symptoms," I said. "Above all—you love to eat, don't you?"

She flushed, then grinned and nodded her head in agreement. I told her that she had been fooling herself about her overweight being caused by an "injection" or a varied assortment of unique "physical problems." I said, "I can't find any physical imbalance or disorder in a thorough examination. Your actual problem is quite common among overweights, a double dilemma: First, you feed your body too much. Second, you exercise your body too little. Simple causes, simple solution. . ."

This patient went on the Quick Teenage Diet and also became more active in her daily living. Her regime, aside from the dieting, included 2 half-hours of brisk walking each day. She said that she was skeptical about this program working for her but promised solemnly that she would give it a faithful one-week trial.

She phoned me a week later, and her voice was so joyous that I could hardly believe it was the same girl. "Doctor," she gurgled, "I've already lost 12 pounds! People are telling me that I look wonderful, that I'm a beautiful girl—but they haven't seen anything yet. I feel like a new person, I'm so full of pep and vigor. I'm going to the store for a new dress in a smaller size than I've worn for years. And yes," she announced, "I'm going to *walk* downtown!"

This young lady stopped in to see me a month later to flaunt her lovely slim figure. Her exquisite heart-shaped face was smiling continuously. I was delighted by the remarkable change in her physically, and in her high spirits. "I know that I'll never be heavy again," she assured me, "since I can always go back on your Quick Teenage Diet if I gain a few pounds. I don't know how to thank you."

Her marvelous transformation was all the thanks I wanted, as with the countless thousands of others I've helped to help themselves. You, too, can and should be among that newly slim number—starting now.

Can Some Eat Limitless Food and Never Gain Weight?

A father said about his whiskered, hairy teenage son whose tresses fell to his shoulders, "That kid never stops eating, and everything he eats seems to turn to hair!" Some overweight youngsters, girls as well as boys, have complained to me along these lines: "Everything I eat turns to fat. I have a skinny friend who eats and eats and eats and it all turns to air, she never gains an ounce." First, I tell such a patient, "Don't burden yourself by thinking about your 'skinny friend' or any other person. Your only overweight problem is yourself."

In the second place, a closer examination proves that the statement is factually untrue. The "skinny person" takes smaller portions, eats different foods, is far more active, doesn't eat as much in calories as appears to be the case. Such individuals seem to know "naturally" when to stop eating. If they gorge themselves one day, they usually eat comparatively little for the next day or two.

On the other hand, visiting in a home, I saw an over-

31

weight girl finish off a dish containing a half-pound of peanuts. Then she complained, "All I had were a few nuts, yet I keep putting on the flab." Actually "all she had" amounted to *hundreds of calories* gobbled up in a few minutes.

Furthermore, the "skinny friend" is usually considerably more active and uses up many more calories per day walking, running, playing, dancing, just moving around. It's certainly true in slimming down that "actions speak louder than words," and a vital part of trimming off the fat and inches is to keep active, to get moving and keep moving around. The fewer the calories eaten, the more calories expended in action, the quicker the pounds disappear.

It all comes down again to intake versus output. You can stuff yourself all day with big portions of low-calorie vegetables and nothing else, and you'll slim down and never be heavy again in your lifetime. But eat a "few" chocolates, cakes, cookies, rolls, spoonfuls of ice cream, nuts, other rich and heavy foods, and large quantities of assorted foods, and you pile up high totals of calories that put on pounds. In addition to that, if you sit around most of the time instead of being on the go, you're not getting rid of many calories through physical activity.

Should You Tell Your Friends You're Dieting?

When you go on the Quick Teenage Diet—and you're starting to diet alone, not with a companion—I suggest that it usually works out best not to talk about it until you've lost 5 to 10 pounds. When you've dropped that weight, generally in just a week, you'll find that your friends are already commenting on your improved appearance. That's a good time to say that you're on a diet. Admitting that you're dieting after others have seen the weight loss is a spur to keep dieting. As the people in the know watch you lose weight and cheer you on, this acts both as a deterrent to going off your diet and an encouragement to further weight loss. Soon you'll be down to the slim, trim look you want—and there will be many more interesting subjects to talk about other than reducing.

If you are going to start your diet at the same time as a friend, or with your sister or brother or the whole family as competition or for teamwork, results are often excellent. The challenge tends to keep you from slipping. If your friend, weighing about the same as you at the start, is losing more weight than you, then you're likely to try a little harder. The competition also helps keep you from cheating. If you're not doing as well as your teammate, you can better analyze your shortcomings and correct them. Soon you'll be losing at the same rate as your overweight friend.

However, if competition upsets you, then diet alone. Individuals differ in temperament and approach. Go at it in the way that's best for you, as long as you get that weight off—that's your all-important goal. In short, you can just go on the Quick Teenage Diet, keep quiet about it except within your own family, and then feel thrilled as others tell you how much slimmer and lovelier you look. (Ask your parents to read Chapter 14, written especially for them.) Or, tell your friends you're on the diet, as a help toward keeping you on the diet and proving that you can do it. Your figure will soon reflect the wonderful results.

WHAT WEIGHT SHOULD YOU BE?

A cartoon shows this scene in a doctor's office: A very heavy young man with bulging stomach and rear is standing on the scale being weighed. The doctor tells

33

him, "No, I wouldn't say you're overweight, but you're one foot, seven inches too short."

The point is that you can become pretty confused trying to figure out exactly to the ounce what you should weigh according to your height measured to the fraction of an inch and your "type" of frame. My basic "weight charts" on following pages are all the guide you need, and will serve you well. Don't waste your time and patience trying to figure your ideal weight to the ounce. Just start the Quick Teenage Diet and slim down in a hurry—the fractions will then take care of themselves.

If you are overweight, you know it very quickly—unless you're intent on kidding yourself. You've seen people try to fake by pulling in their stomachs when they're asked their weight. Girls may attempt to conceal a bulging abdomen with loose-fitting clothes. But why fool yourself? A quick look in the mirror at your unclothed body, or the way you appear in a bathing suit, is enough to tell you whether you should take off some pounds and inches. My weight chart pins down the figures accurately enough for you personally. That's the number you should head for as you diet and note the pounds diminishing on the scale day after day.

You'll find that the figures on my chart are lower than most of the "average" weight tables printed elsewhere. Those "average" numbers include the enormous percentage of the population, teenage and adult, who are overweight. Therefore the "averages" are too high for the maximum health and attractiveness you want, from my viewpoint. My "ideal" weight numbers are worked out to help keep you feeling tops, living healthier and longer than you would with excess poundage, and looking your best.

The numbers on my chart are for the unclothed figure. Weigh yourself nude on the bathroom scale soon after you arise and before you eat each morning.

How to Find Your Proper Weight

Select the weight chart that applies to you ("female weight chart" or "male weight chart"). According to your age, go down the proper column to your height, to determine your desired weight. The lower figure is your "ideal weight"—the higher figure is about "average weight." You can choose the weight about midway between the two figures as your "desired weight," depending on whether you tend to be small-boned or large-boned.

FEMALE: As an example, if you are age 17, and 5′ 4″ tall, your ideal weight would be 100 lbs., ranging up to 112 lbs. average weight, on the chart. Figuring about midway, 106 lbs. would be about your desired weight. I recommend *ideal weight*, about 100 lbs. in this instance, as the most healthful guide for girls in general at this age and height.

MALE: For example, if you are age 15, and 5′ 8″ in height, your ideal weight would be 130 lbs., ranging to about 144 lbs. average weight. Figuring about midway, 137 lbs. would be about your desired weight. I recommend *ideal weight*, about 130 lbs. in this instance, as the most healthful guide for boys in general at this age and height.

FEMALES: General Rule to Figure Weight

Start with 100 lbs. for 5′ tall; add 3½ lbs. for each inch of your height over 5′—that's about the *"average"* weight. Now deduct 1 lb. for every year between your age and 25—that's about your *"ideal"* weight. Your *"desired"* weight is about midway between "average" and "ideal."

For example, if you are 5′ 4″ tall, you start with 100 lbs., plus 4″ x 3½ lbs., or 14 lbs.—a total of about 114 lbs. "average" weight. If you are age 14, deduct 14 from 25—that's 11 lbs. off 114 and figures to about 103 lbs.

FEMALE WEIGHT CHART

Height	Age 13	14	15	16	17	18	19
5'	85-90	85-90	85-90	86-91	87-92	88-93	89-94
5' 1"	85-93	85-94	85-95	86-96	87-97	88-98	89-99
5' 2"	88-98	89-99	90-100	91-101	92-102	93-103	94-104
5' 3"	91-103	92-104	93-105	94-106	95-107	96-108	97-109
5' 4"	96-108	97-109	98-110	99-111	100-112	101-113	102-114
5' 5"	100-113	101-114	102-115	103-116	104-117	105-118	106-119
5' 6"	105-118	106-119	107-120	108-121	109-122	110-123	111-124
5' 7"	109-123	110-124	111-125	112-126	113-127	114-128	115-129
5' 8"	112-128	113-129	114-130	115-131	116-132	117-133	118-134
5' 9"	118-133	119-134	120-135	121-136	122-137	123-138	124-139
5' 10"	123-138	124-139	125-140	126-141	127-142	128-143	129-144
5' 11"	128-143	129-144	130-145	131-146	132-147	133-148	134-149
6'	132-148	133-149	134-150	135-151	136-152	137-153	138-154
6' 1"	136-153	137-154	138-155	139-156	140-157	141-158	142-159
6' 2"	141-158	142-159	143-160	144-161	145-162	146-163	147-164

"ideal" weight. Your "desired" weight would be about midway between 114 lbs. and 103 lbs.—that comes to about 108 lbs. (I recommend closer to the "ideal" weight figure for most teenagers.) The final figure may vary from the chart a few pounds one way or the other, since no "general" rule can apply to each individual, but it will be close enough to serve as a good general guide for you (check your unclothed figure in the mirror).

Females: Calories per Day to Maintain Desired Weight

To maintain your desired weight, once you're down to it by dieting, multiply each pound of total weight by 12 to arrive at the number of calories per day approximately that will keep you at that weight.

For example, if your desired weight is 110 lbs., multiply 110 x 12, for a total of 1,300 to 1,350 calories per day generally to keep you at that weight. If you find you are gaining with that calorie count, decrease your calorie intake a little. If losing weight, increase your calorie intake a bit until you arrive at the correct amount to maintain desired weight for yourself.

MALES: General Rule to Figure Weight

Start with 100 lbs. for 5' tall; add 5 lbs. for each inch of your height over 5'—that's about "*average*" weight. Now deduct 1 lb. for every year between your age and 25—that's about your "*ideal*" weight. Your "*desired*" weight is about midway between "average" and "ideal."

For example, if you are 5' 4" tall, you start with 100 lbs., plus 4" x 5 lbs., or 20 lbs.—a total of 120 lbs. "average" weight. If you are age 14, deduct 14 from 25— that's 11 lbs. off 120 and figures to about 109 lbs. "ideal" weight. Your "desired" weight would be about midway

MALE WEIGHT CHART

Height	Age 13	14	15	16	17	18	19
5′	93-98	94-99	95-100	96-101	97-102	98-103	99-104
5′1″	93-101	94-102	95-103	96-104	97-105	98-106	99-109
5′2″	98-109	99-110	100-111	101-112	102-113	103-114	104-115
5′3″	101-114	102-115	103-116	104-117	105-118	106-119	107-120
5′4″	108-120	109-121	110-122	111-123	112-124	113-125	114-126
5′5″	111-125	112-126	113-127	114-128	115-129	116-130	117-131
5′6″	118-131	119-132	120-133	121-134	122-135	123-136	124-137
5′7″	121-136	122-137	123-138	124-139	125-140	126-141	127-142
5′8″	128-142	129-143	130-144	131-145	132-146	133-147	134-148
5′9″	131-147	132-148	133-149	134-150	135-151	136-152	137-153
5′10″	138-153	139-154	140-155	141-156	142-157	143-158	144-159
5′11″	141-157	142-158	143-159	144-160	145-161	146-162	147-163
6′	148-164	149-165	150-166	151-167	152-168	153-169	154-170
6′1″	151-169	152-170	153-171	154-172	155-173	156-174	157-175
6′2″	158-175	159-176	160-177	161-178	162-179	163-180	164-181

between 120 lbs. and 109 lbs.—that comes to about 115 lbs. (I recommend closer to the "ideal" weight figure for most teenagers.) The final figure may vary from the chart a few pounds one way or the other, since no "general" rule can apply to each individual, but it will be close enough to serve as a good general guide for you (check your unclothed figure in the mirror).

Males: Calories per Day to Maintain Desired Weight

To maintain your desired weight, once you're down to it by dieting, multiply each pound of total weight by 13 to arrive at the number of calories per day approximately that will keep you at that weight.

For example, if your desired weight is 140 lbs., multiply 140 x 13, for a total of 1,800 to 1,850 calories per day generally to keep you at that weight. If you find that you are gaining with that calorie count, decrease your calorie intake a little. If losing weight, increase your calorie intake a bit until you arrive at the correct amount to maintain desired weight for yourself.

Exercise Affects Daily Calorie Intake

"Daily calorie intake" means the number of calories in food on an average daily to keep you at your ideal weight. However, if you are an individual, whether boy or girl, who gets little exercise and activity, the daily total may change. If you find yourself gaining weight on your "daily calorie maintenance total," cut 300 to 500 calories daily from the total. That should take care of not using up enough calories through normal exercise and activity. It is better for your health and well-being, of course, if you do increase your activity and thus use up calories

by energetic walking, or through sports, or whatever you prefer.

The daily calorie totals suggested for you are not particularly low, though they may seem low compared with some "average weight" calorie totals provided by some others. It's of interest to note that at teenage "reducing camps," the average daily diet is limited to 950–1,150 calories generally, and a good deal of exercise and activity is included in the daily program as a "must."

Physical Differences in Teenagers

There are enormous variations in height for each age, during the teenage years particularly. Measurements of hundreds of campers show differences of up to 10 and more inches among both boys and girls of each teenage year. In one camp, for example, boys of age 14 ranged from 52" to 67" tall; at age 15 from 56" to 69" tall; at age 18 from 62" to 72" tall; and so on. Girls ranged in height at age 13 from 53" to 68"; at age 15 from 57" to 69"; at age 18 from 60" to 70"; and so on.

The primary point to keep in mind is this: Your good health and ideal weight for your personal height at each stage are what are most important, not how short or tall you happen to be. If you are at all concerned about being too short or too tall at any age, be sure to see your doctor for reassurance and guidance or treatment. (Have an annual checkup by a physician each year, no matter what.)

Realize that most teenagers are adolescents, and physical factors are to be judged accordingly. Adolescence means no more in general than "growing up." During the adolescent spurt, an individual can grow 1 millimeter in 4 days, 1 centimeter in 40 days. Translated into inches, this means about 1" in 100 days, as much as 3½" in one year. Again, this varies with each person.

Most youngsters have a spurt of 2½" to 3½" in some

one year, then less in following years. Some keep growing 2″ to 3″ in height over a period of 4 to 8 years. While growth in height is likely to stop after age 18, medical researchers have found that some young men may gain up to 1″ after age 18, and some young women may gain ½″ to ¾″ after 18 years of age.

The end of adolescence is by definition the time when growth in height ceases (but not growth in muscle and fat). The end of growth in height usually occurs at age 17 to 18 for girls, and age 18 to 20 for boys. However, the increased growth in muscle and fat continues, and even the bone width may increase in size. Just aim to be at ideal weight at every age in your adolescence, and for the rest of your life.

Since no two individuals are exactly alike, nor function in precisely the same way, don't be too concerned if you don't attain exactly the "ideal weight" as figured by my earlier instructions or by the weight chart. A difference of 5 to 10 pounds more than my ideal weight figure may be all right for you, according to your individual frame and characteristics. A few more pounds may be right for you as long as you look slim and trim, with an attractive figure for your height.

Other Ideal Weight Guides

Check your height carefully, in bare feet or wearing socks, before figuring out your personal ideal weight. Doctors find that boys tend to estimate their height at a few inches taller than it actually is, whereas taller girls tend to give lower than accurate figures.

Don't be concerned about "frame" category. I purposely don't give different figures for "small, medium, large frame." My reason is that invariably overweights of any age will take the greater "large frame" figures as the guide, even though most have medium or small

41

frames. Use my ideal weight numbers as your basic personal guide to achieve a slim, trim, healthy figure.

Realize that there are many variations worldwide according to geographical area, country of origin, race, and other differences. Don't be concerned if you're not "average" in height according to your age. Reaching and maintaining the ideal slim, trim weight for your height and age is the primary consideration for good health and long life . . . all other factors being equal.

Don't consider my ideal weight figures as too low. As one basis for comparison, I studied the weight figures for winners of some female beauty contests during recent years. The figures varied considerably but, in general, the winners, either teenage or a few years older, were about *5 to 10 pounds or more under the ideal weight figures provided as your guide.* Compare:

New York State beauty pageant contestants averaged 5′ 5″ in height and 115 pounds in weight (rather than 123–128 ideal weight chart figures).

Miss Teenager beauty contest winner was 5′ 6″ tall and weighed 118 pounds.

Miss America: 5′ 6″ tall, 119 pounds.

Miss U.S.A.: 5′ 7″ tall, 121 pounds.

Miss Universe: 5′ 8″ tall, 123 pounds.

There's food for thought (not for digestion) for you in the fact that these young women, rated by judges as having "ideal" figures, were in general about 5 to 10 pounds *under* my ideal weight guide. Don't let anyone get away with telling you that my standards for you are too severe, or the weights too low. My personal examinations of over 10,000 teenagers support my recommendations as correct (if anything, I would tend to lower my listed ideal weight figures rather than increase them).

A study of 2,000 teenage boys which I conducted over the past few years revealed some facts of significance to teenagers of both sexes. I compared 1,000 tall and lanky boys with 1,000 stocky overweights.

The tall boys, average age 17 years, averaged 6 feet in

height and 140 pounds in weight. According to most "average weight" tables, these young men would have averaged 175 pounds—so, judging by these figures, the boys averaged 35 *pounds underweight.* According to my ideal weight table, the ideal weight for these young men would be about 150 pounds—so, according to this standard, they were about 10 pounds underweight. My examinations showed that they were alert, active, excellent at sports, in extremely good health. Thus, being a little underweight, even according to my basic chart, is desirable rather than otherwise.

The stocky boys, average age 17, averaged 5' 9½" in height and 189 pounds in weight. According to most "average weight" tables, they should have weighed about 155 pounds—so by these standards they were about 35 *pounds overweight.* Looking at my height-weight guide, their ideal weight should be about 140 pounds, so I consider them about 50 *pounds overweight.* I found these overweight young men comparatively inactive, lethargic, and not nearly in as good condition as the lanky, underweight 17-year-olds.

My findings with teenage girls are similar, that they are far better off in every way being a little underweight than overweight. The slim ones are as a whole better in general health, in appearance, in alertness, and in physical and mental activities, emotionally and socially.

Teenagers who are highly exercised athletes, other than sprinters, tend to be up to 8 to 10 pounds heavier (girls less than boys) than the average ideal weight according to my figures. That's because of above-average muscular development, with the added muscles increasing the total weight. Yet the many teenage athletes I examined would be considered *underweight* by most of the "average weight-height" tables. Nevertheless these boys and girls had exceptional vigor and stamina.

Warning to teenage boys: Don't strive to be a "muscle man" like those pictured in physical-culture photos. If you are considerably overweight because of muscle rather than fat, your heart and other organs still have to support those extra pounds of weight, each ounce part of the demanding circulatory system. Findings show repeatedly that considerably overweight "muscle men" have very poor health and longevity records.

As teenagers grow taller, females as well as males, it becomes increasingly important to be slim and trim. Compared with teenagers a generation ago, height is on the increase. But for those who grow taller than average, this is significant—medical findings indicate that the heart doesn't grow in proportion to the increased height. The heart works harder to pump blood through the taller frame; therefore it becomes even more important to be at ideal weight or a few pounds underweight in order to relieve the heart from also pumping blood to support excess fat.

Use your common sense and the figure reflected by your mirror as additional guides. The long and short of it is this: Whether you're tall, average size, or short . . . whatever type of frame you have . . . "ideal weight" or a little under is the healthiest weight for you.

And if you are overweight, concentrate on getting rid of your excess pounds in a hurry, pound after pound, and day after day—on my Quick Teenage Diet or one of the variations of your personal choice. What really counts is arriving as speedily as possible at the great day when you see your slim, attractive figure in the mirror. Slenderness may not ensure happiness—but it sure helps.

3

Why Pounds and Inches Vanish Speedily on the Quick Teenage Diet

An overweight teenager who had failed time after time to reduce on a variety of calorie-counting diets said, "I'm getting to the point that I think even the polluted air I'm breathing is loaded with calories." My Quick Teenage Diet eliminates all that calorie confusion for you. That's just one of the reasons why you're likely to succeed with this dieting method although you've failed on others.

Instead of counting calories (which do count, as I explain repeatedly in these pages), you eat well, enough to satisfy in moderate portions, from a list of excellent protein foods. You enjoy all kinds of lean meats, fish, seafood, chicken and turkey, eggs, cottage cheese. You'll find that the instructions are clear, simple, very easy to follow.

You start to lose weight at once. You don't have to wait a week in hopes that 1 pound or 2 will vanish from your body. On the Quick Teenage Diet, you'll see your weight dropping within a day or two, and day after day thereafter.

Rapid weight loss is the "built-in will power" that's such a vital part of successful reducing. Where there's will power, there's weight-loss power. You gain the sustaining drive to keep dieting when you have the incentive of daily weight loss.

You'll lose 5, 10, 15 or more pounds a week by following the simple directions exactly. How much you lose depends on how much over ideal weight you are, and how faithfully you stick to the diet instructions. The more excess weight you have, the more will come off quickly. In general, you'll lose 5 percent to 10 percent of your total weight the first week.

This letter from a very heavy teenage girl is typical of what happens: "I've been on your diet for only two weeks and have lost 23 pounds. It's great . . . I started at 281 pounds, and wow! I've been on hundreds of diets that promised a loss of 10 pounds a week or better, but they all failed me badly. . . You're the only one who has ever been able to take off my fat bulges. . . Thanks to you, I'll live 20 years longer and go with the boys I've liked for years but had to avoid. . . Thank you sincerely from an ex-fat-slob on the right road to recovery!"

You lose weight rapidly week after week on the Quick Teenage Diet. You lose about 5 pounds or more per week on the average—with a greater loss the first week, again depending on how much excess fat you're carrying. It's very easy to figure out that if you're 5 pounds overweight, you should get down to your ideal weight within a week without any question. If you're 10 pounds too heavy, you should lose the excess in less than 2 weeks. You'll take off 15 pounds in two to three weeks, and so on.

Very heavy teenagers have lost over 20 pounds the first week on my Quick Teenage Diet in my experience. They have done this healthfully, feeling stronger rather than weaker for having shed the burden of all those excess pounds. Spurred by the wonderful first-week improvement in their figures and in that marvelous new feeling of lightness, many have gone on joyfully to lose 50 and more pounds in as little as two months, an accomplishment they had never before dreamed was possible.

You can lose weight in stages if you are very heavy and have a long way to go. For example, a typical overweight teenage girl in my care lost 28 pounds in three weeks on rapid weight-loss dieting, dropping from 170 pounds to 142. She then went on Keep-Slim Eating (see Chapter 11, on that subject) for two weeks, remaining at about 142. She went back to the Quick Teenage Diet, dieting for a few more weeks and dropping 20 more pounds to 122.

After two weeks on Keep-Slim Eating, retaining that weight on the scale, she dieted two more weeks until she lost 10 more pounds and was down to her ideal weight, a slim, trim 112 pounds. After that, following the rules of Keep-Slim Eating, she never went higher than 115 pounds, ranging between 110 and 115 week after week. Her spirit was more than willing, once her weight started dropping, and her excess flesh vanished. You can accomplish the same.

You won't be on the Quick Teenage Diet "forever." I don't recommend that you stay on this protein-eating method for the rest of your life, even though most people could live healthfully ever after in this way. My instructions are to shift to the Keep-Slim method of eating a variety of foods, and you'll remain slim as long as you don't exceed the calorie limitation for your ideal weight.

It becomes easier to eat less, usually after a few days on the Quick Teenage Diet. You learn a new way of eating: that is, eating to sustain yourself rather than to stuff and overstuff your gullet and your belly. You not only adopt a new attitude about the relative *un*importance of food, you adopt eagerly to a new, better way of living. Food will become the least important measure of "pleasure" in your young life, and hopefully and healthfully, for the rest of your years.

Follow the lead of people in the public spotlight. Many young actors and actresses, and others in the public eye, use my speedy reducing methods to slim down for the camera's eye at first, and then again and again. A movie starlet said, "Your rapid reducing method is part of my glamorous way of life since I just can't afford to get chubby." A young writer told me, "When I'm going for a TV interview, I realize that the camera tends to make me look heavier. Even though I'm at my desired

47

weight, a few days before going on TV I go on the Quick Teenage Diet and trim off 3 or 4 pounds so I'll look slim and fit on the TV tube."

A beautiful young actress informed me, "Your speedy reducing methods practically saved my life. After my show closed, I went to a resort for a week, loafed around and over-ate, gaining 7 pounds. My agent phoned and said he'd set up an audition for me a week later. I almost panicked because I looked so pudgy. I went on the Quick Teenage Diet and took off the 7 pounds before the week was over. Your dieting method is a life-saver for me!"

Beware the "3-pounds-over danger signal." I suggest that you weigh yourself every morning, undressed, before breakfast, even after you're down to your ideal weight and back to "normal" eating. If you find any day that you're 3 pounds over your desired weight, go right back on the Quick Teenage Diet for a couple of days to get rid of those excess pounds. Do it immediately, lest the pounds pile on, as they have a tendency to do with people gaining weight.

Certainly once you are slim you'll go on occasional eating binges—weekends, parties, holidays, vacations. That's fine, as long as you don't let the overweight stay and increase. Quick action always with the Quick Teenage Diet will bring you right back to your right weight. Don't worry about up-and-down weight being unhealthy —it isn't. You can see-saw safely, as long as you come down, and don't stay up there above ideal weight.

You have a handy reducing method forever. With the Quick Teenage Diet, and my other speedy-reducing methods, you have a "tool" to help you stay thin always. If your weight goes up after a big-eating holiday, take it right off with the Quick Teenage Diet. Pounds increased after graduation festivities? Back you go on the Quick Teenage Diet to trim down immediately. You'll never again in your life be at a loss for the sure way to lose pounds swiftly, healthfully, pleasantly.

How S.D.A.—Specific Dynamic Action—Slims You Quicker

This method of dieting, using S.D.A., the specific dynamic action of protein, is exceptionally well suited to you as a teenager, as it burns up fat 18 percent to 50 percent better than "balanced" diets rich in carbohydrates. This feature ties in with other youthful advantages —a faster metabolism generally, a physically more active way of living than that of many older people. All these pluses help you take off pounds rapidly when you stay on the Quick Teenage Diet faithfully, with no overeating *anything*, and no snacking on non-protein foods.

I have found that most teenagers have a sizable bump of scientific curiosity. You want to know not only that a certain course of action—following the Quick Teenage Diet in this instance—*will* produce certain results, but also *how* and *why*. The explanation that follows doesn't go into all the intricate details that only a scientist would comprehend. It does provide a basis for understanding what happens within you when you go on the Quick Teenage Diet. You may skip this explanation if you wish.

The fact is that this way of dieting *burns up more calories* than diets consisting of a variety of foods totaling the same caloric intake. In other words, if you consume 1,300 calories daily on the Quick Teenage Diet— compared with 1,300 calories daily of an assortment of foods including sugar, sweets, breads, any carbohydrates —you'll burn up about *200 to 500 or more calories daily* on the Quick Teenage Diet. The result is as if you ate about 200 to 500 fewer calories that day.

Some researchers state that pure protein may be up to 50 percent more effective in cutting calories—that is, 1,300 calories in variety foods would be equivalent in effect to 650 calories in all-protein foods. If you eat less on QTD, perhaps 1,000 calories, you would then be getting only 500 calories comparably according to the 50 percent measure. A European doctor claims that one can never be overweight with pure protein eating, no matter how much you eat, but I don't subscribe to that. Just follow my Quick Teenage Diet exactly, and you'll have no problems in losing weight with remarkable speed, comfort, and high energy.

The reason for the more efficient burning of fat is that the foods listed for you are practically all protein. When you eat these foods only, as instructed, your system benefits from the S.D.A., specific dynamic action, of protein. From a chemical and metabolic viewpoint, S.D.A. burns up fat more efficiently than other types of food generally eaten, on varied common diets containing an assortment of foods including carbohydrates, for instance—cookies, cakes, fruits, vegetables, oils, margarine, butter.

For each pound of fat that is burned by the human system for energy, the body also loses about 1¼ pounds of water. But there is a still greater loss of fat and water on the Quick Teenage Diet due to the S.D.A. of protein. If 1,000 calories are taken in, the higher amount of "heat" produced by the protein S.D.A. would cut the calories to about 750 or even 500 calories in effect. The body loses more fat and more water, easily losing 5 or more pounds per week. Naturally, the fewer calories you eat, the quicker you lose pounds and inches.

Most of the foods that grow have some protein in them. Thus they are able to raise "the fires of metabolism" to some extent, how much depending on the amount of protein ingested. The foods you eat on the Quick Teenage Diet being practically all protein, your system "burns up" your own excess fat more effectively. This helps you lose weight more speedily.

Your body is not without sugar while on QTD, because some of your own body fat, as your system functions, is converted into a small percentage of carbohydrate or sugar. The rest of the fat is converted into fuel or energy. Mainly the fat is broken down in the "burning" into fatty acids that provide the body with its energy and heat even though no sizable amounts of sugars or carbohydrates are eaten. It all combines for an efficient step-by-step action and reaction, and with each reaction some essential heat and energy are slowly produced.

I could go on in considerable detail, but it's not necessary in order for you to lose weight quickly and surely—and that's what concerns you primarily. Studies have shown that individuals, male and female, on a high-protein diet such as the Quick Teenage Diet, *melt the fat out of the storage or fat centers more effectively,* and therefore lose weight more rapidly than on a comparable calorie intake of varied foods.

If you break the diet, and eat sugars and carbohydrates instead of the high-protein foods specified, the body bypasses using your fat and uses the carbohydrates instead. In that manner, the fat is stored in your fat depots instead of being burned up. Therefore it is most important that you eat only the foods listed for the Quick Teenage Diet.

While the specific dynamic action of protein burns up fat more rapidly, your body is not deprived of any essential elements while you're on the Quick Teenage Diet—as explained, you don't stay on the diet "forever." That marvelous mechanism that is your body uses up and converts its own fat into elements required for healthful functioning.

On this high-protein eating, the body not only loses extra fat but also withdraws extra intercellular water, inducing more frequent urination. As the result of the fat and water loss, your body is lighter. The heart beats more easily. The lungs breathe, and blood flows more readily.

Combining this dominantly protein way of eating on the Quick Teenage Diet with increased activity, exercise, and ease of movement, you soon reflect the wonderful, healthful change in many ways. You're headed immediately, you know for sure, toward the slimming, trimming success you're seeking.

Please understand that I don't claim that high-protein diets are "new" or a "miracle" or so-called "fad" of my creation. Nor did I devise S.D.A., the specific dynamic action of protein; this is a well-known scientific organic function (although science hasn't fully solved all the why's and wherefore's of the digestive process). It is my application of the scientific facts that has broken the frustration barrier in dieting. The Quick Teenage Diet is different because it is practically an *all*-protein rather than just high-protein diet.

Don't Ever Be Discouraged

Now that you know in a very general way how the specific dynamic action can work for you to lose weight rapidly, use it right now and for the rest of your life whenever reducing is necessary. If you suddenly find yourself "falling off the S.D.A." by snacking on sweets or other high-carbohydrate foods, don't despair. Don't kick yourself around—that's a waste of time and emotion, accomplishing nothing. I remind you that you're not the first to slip, and you won't be the last.

Simply shrug off any discouragement and go right back on the Quick Teenage Diet. You'll be starting S.D.A. working for you all over again, and it will start reducing you swiftly. Disraeli said, "The secret of success is constancy to purpose." I assure you that some of the greatest dieting successes have sprouted from a series of failures. *The diet works*—its up to you to give it at least one week's trial.

4

The Proved Quick Teenage Diet

You don't have to "guess" or "hope" that the Quick Teenage Diet will take off the pounds and inches you want to lose—*you know that it will work for you* because it has reduced so many others who had failed with other dieting methods. My book for overweight adults, *"The Doctor's Quick Weight Loss Diet,"* became the bestselling reducing book of all time—over 5,000,000 copies sold at this writing, over two years on bestseller lists and still going strong, published in a number of languages and different countries around the world (overweight is unwanted in any language!).

The all-important point to you is that this record-breaking success of my speedy-reducing methods is due to one reason: *the diet works.*

QTD ... THE QUICK TEENAGE DIET

The following are the foods that you eat—all wholesome all-protein foods plus 1 or 2 glasses of skim milk per day.

You make up your meals from the listing of foods that follow, with no need to go through a catalog of all the foods in the world for your daily selection.

You don't have to count calories, since the items listed are selected primarily to give you healthful food values along with the quick-reducing benefits of S.D.A., the specific dynamic action of protein.

You simply select from the listed foods, and don't add any others until you've reduced to your ideal weight through the Quick Teenage Diet (unless you're extremely overweight and take off the pounds in stages).

You don't have to measure out or weigh your food in ounces on the regular Quick Teenage Diet (you may if you choose the Super-Quick Teenage Diets given in the next chapter). You simply eat small-to-moderate portions —not large or excessive servings—of the foods listed.

You make up your meals according to your own choice from these foods:

■ SKIM MILK. Up to age 18 (through age 17), 2 glasses (8-oz.) of skim milk per day are recommended. From age 18 on, 1 glass (8-oz.) of skim milk per day is sufficient.

Skim milk is desirable in the Quick Teenage Diet because it provides additional calcium, whch is needed by the growng teenager. On QTD you also get calcium from cottage cheese, pot cheese, and farmer cheese, and some calcium from salmon, sardines, oysters, and many other protein foods in combination.

Because of calorie content, and the importance of keeping calorie intake at a minimum on any reducing diet, make sure to use skim milk in cartons or bottles, or powdered nonfat dry milk (mixed with water as per package directions). Don't use whole milk or "99% Non-Fat Milk." You get all the beneficial elements in the skim milks without the undesirable fat—and with only about half the calories of whole milk. Note the tremendous difference in calorie content as given by one leading producer of many milk products, per 8-oz. glass:

Skim milk .... 80 calories
Powdered nonfat dry milk .... 80 "
"99% Non-Fat Milk" .... 115 "
Whole milk .... 150 "
   (Some whole milk is up to 165 calories)

It's essential to use skim milk instead of whole milk for 2 reasons: First, you get the slimming benefits of 70 calories saved per 8-ounce glass. Second, you eliminate the fat that would interfere with the most efficient functioning of the specific dynamic action of protein.

Don't use as an excuse perhaps that you don't like the taste of skim milk as compared with whole milk. After a day or so of switching to skim milk, you'll become accustomed to it. Many people who switch to skim milk and then try whole milk some time later say that they can't stand whole milk because of its "fatty taste."

If you wish, you may add non-caloric artificially sweetened flavorings, whichever ones you prefer personally, to the skim milk.

If, because of an allergy, or for any other reason, you can't drink milk at all, don't worry about it. (Some people who are allergic to milk find that they avoid the allergic reaction by boiling the milk before drinking; boiled milk is a coagulated protein, and usually is not allergenic.)

Good health doesn't depend on drinking milk. However, you should have the daily calcium equivalent, so take the "normal daily requirements" in calcium tablets (see label directions on whatever brand you get) if you don't drink milk. In addition, as noted before, your body is getting some calcium from other foods on QTD.

Drink the milk at any time of the day you wish, with meals or between meals, the full 8-ounce glass each time, or divided into smaller portions. However, because of calorie content, don't have more than 1 or 2 glasses per day specified, according to your age.

■ LEAN MEATS. You may have lean beef, lamb, or veal (no ham or pork, since while these are nutritious foods, they are higher in calories and therefore not recommended on the diet—save the ham and pork products for Keep-Slim Eating). In preparing and eating the lean meats, all visible fats should be removed before cooking, and then again before eating. The meats should be broiled, baked, or boiled—never fried. In preparing, cooking, and eating meats, don't use any butter, margarine, oils, or any other fats. You may use practically any herbs, spices, and other mild seasonings that you wish in preparing, cooking, and eating the lean meats. Don't have any gravy or sauces on your meat.

Variety meats are permitted when broiled. These include beef liver, calf's liver, kidneys, sweetbreads, and other such meats if you want them. Be sure to remove any visible fats before cooking and when eating. Don't use any butter, margarine, oils, or any other fats in preparing or eating. If the prepared variety meats look at all greasy, pat them dry with a paper towel or napkin.

Frankfurters are allowed on the diet, but only all-beef frankfurters (containing no pork or high-calorie fillers, no carbohydrate or cereal fillings). Prepare the frankfurters broiled or boiled, slicing in half lengthwise before broiling. When cooked, pat the frankfurters with a paper towel or napkin to remove all fat drippings. They may be eaten with a little mustard or ketchup, but only a little—don't pile on the mustard or ketchup, or you'll impede the most efficient functioning of the specific dynamic action of protein on QTD.

Smoked meats are permitted, with restrictions, but only all-beef products (no pork content or high-calorie fillers), and not highly spiced brands. The types allowed include all-beef bologna, corned beef, pastrami, tongue—but note the following limitations. Eat only small to moderate portions, never big portions. Trim off any visible fat before preparing and eating—very important on corned beef, pastrami, and tongue especially. *Broil* any of the smoked meats, including all-beef bologna, and pat off the fat drippings with a paper towel or paper napkin before eating.

If your doctor has ever told you that you have a tendency toward high blood pressure (increasingly common

56

among teenagers as well as adults), or that you are a "water retainer," I advise that you do without smoked or other salted foods—no salty or smoked meats, fish, or other highly spiced foods (this applies to salty foods only; pure spices or condiments are all right).

■ CHICKEN, TURKEY. Enjoy chicken and turkey, white meat and dark meat (but never any meat in large quantities)—broiled, roasted, or boiled. All skin should be removed, preferably before preparation and cooking, and certainly before eating (the skin is high in fat and calories, very undesirable). When boiling chicken, all fat should be skimmed off repeatedly. In cooking, don't use any butter, margarine, oils, or any other fats. In eating, don't use any gravy or sauces.

"Turkey Roll" and *"Chicken Roll,"* when lean and not highly spiced, are permitted in small-to-moderate portions, smaller if dark meat, which contains more calories than light meat.

Smoked turkey and smoked chicken tend to be spicy and fatty and should be avoided, especially if you have any tendency toward high blood pressure or water-retention.

■ LEAN FISH. You may eat practically any fresh or frozen (not smoked) fish in moderate portions, after removing skin and any visible fat. It should be broiled, baked, or boiled, never fried. Don't use any butter, margarine, oils, or fats of any kind. Don't use any sauces, other than a little (never a lot) of ketchup or chili sauce. Squeezing a little fresh lemon juice over the fish is also permitted.

Canned salmon, tuna, sardines. These are good protein foods for the Quick Teenage Diet, but either get the cans with labels marked "water packed" (packed in water instead of in oil), or drain off the oil in the regular types. You can let all the oil run off, then pat off the fish with a paper towel to remove as much more oil as possible. Or, empty the can in a large sieve and hold the food under slowly running water until all possible oil is washed off—and then pat dry with a paper towel. If a forkful still tastes oily, skip the rest, as the oil adds many calories and interferes with the most speedy reducing power of the Quick Teenage Diet. For added flavor it's all right to squeeze a little fresh lemon juice on the salmon, tuna, or sardines.

The same advice applies to other tinned fish and seafood; get the kind labeled "packed in water," rather than the usual type that's packed in oil. Some people say that they much prefer the water-packed types after a while because they come to dislike anything with an "oily taste." Whether water-packed fish tastes better to you or not, one thing is sure, it's better for you, with many fewer calories, and the reduction in oil content is an aid to a better complexion. If necessary to pep up the flavor, use freshly squeezed lemon juice as advised, a dash of salt, a little vinegar, or a bit of low-calorie dressing, but never a creamy type.

Smoked fish. While on QTD, don't eat any smoked fish such as smoked haddock, kippered herring, assorted herrings, smoked salmon, sturgeon, or whitefish. In most cases, the rich smoked fishes have about *double* the calories per portion of fresh fish, and much more unwanted oils and fats. Skip smoked fish completely while you're slimming.

■ SEAFOOD. Practically all the common seafoods can be included on QTD, since they're low in calories and high in protein, such as clams, crabs, crab legs, lobsters, lobster tails, oysters, prawns, scallops, shrimps. Eat them only broiled, baked, or boiled—never fried, neither pan-fried nor deep-fat-fried, nor prepared with high-calorie ingredients (as in making deviled crab cakes). Don't use any oils, butter, margarine, or any other high-calorie additives in cooking or eating.

Canned seafood is permitted on QTD if water-packed, such as plain minced clams, pre-cooked steamed clams, and pure clam juice. Examine the labels carefully, and don't use the contents if any oils are included.

Smoked seafood, such as smoked oysters, should not be eaten on this diet. Calorie content is relatively high in smoked seafood, and the added fats and oils used in preparation cut down on the effectiveness of the reducing process.

You can use a small amount of cocktail sauce, ketchup, chili sauce, vinegar, lemon juice, or non-creamy low-calorie dressings on seafood—but don't ever use large quantities of such sauces or dressings.

■ EGGS. As an excellent source of protein, you may enjoy eggs cooked in any way that doesn't use butter, margarine, oil, bacon fat, or any other fats. Hard-boiled eggs are recommended particularly; you may also have soft or medium boiled, poached, or fried, scrambled, or omelet-style in a non-stick no-fat pan. It's helpful to prepare some extra hard-boiled eggs to keep handy in the refrigerator for meals or a special between-meals snack.

■ COTTAGE CHEESE. This is a fine food for the Quick Teenage Diet, as it is high in protein and also contains calcium and other beneficial elements. It may be used in many satisfying variations, such as mixed with cinnamon and artificial sweetener . . . with a little lemon, vanilla, or other flavoring . . . with minced clams as a luncheon or dinner dish . . . mixed with eggs for scrambling . . . and other recipes that you can create for yourself from the items permitted on the diet. Many successful QTD dieters like cottage cheese plain or flavored by adding a little salt, artificial sweetener, or herbs, spices, or other no-calorie seasoning to taste.

Choose from various types of cottage cheese, according to your personal preferences. *Creamed cottage cheese* is the most popular and most readily available cottage cheese, and the most used by successful quick weight-loss dieters. In the processing, a very small amount of skim milk or whole milk is added for moistness, but not enough milk to interfere with the efficient working of the specific dynamic action of protein in taking off your excess pounds quickly.

"*Skim-milk cottage cheese*" and "*diet cottage cheese*" are available in some stores. These are very good, moist and tasty, and you may prefer to use them instead of "creamed cottage cheese" in order to cut calories further in your daily eating.

Pot cheese is cottage cheese without any milk added, again saving some calories compared with "creamed cottage cheese." Some dieters prefer its relatively dry texture; the choice is up to you.

Farmer cheese is cottage cheese pressed into a bar for cutting into slices or cubes, as you prefer it, and is a great favorite with many teenagers as a change from other forms of cottage cheese. There is no milk added, so farmer cheese has a few less calories than creamed cottage cheese. Farmer cheese may not be available in your area or in all stores.

Most other cheeses are not suitable for the Quick Teenage Diet, since they contain too much milk or cream. If you can find other types of cheese in stores labeled "made with skim milk," you may eat them on QTD. However, most so-called skim milk cheeses are actually labeled "made with part skim milk," and you never know what percentage of added milk is skim, whole milk, or cream. I recommend that while you are on QTD, to lose pounds most rapidly, you should confine your cheese-eating to one of the forms of cottage cheese, except for a little mozzarella cheese occasionally.

■ VITAMIN-MINERAL TABLET EVERY DAY. You are to take a vitamin-mineral supplement every day that you are on the Quick Teenage Diet. Choose any form you wish that provides on the label "average daily vitamin-mineral requirements." You may take tablets, capsules, pills, liquids, as you please. Actually I have never found anyone to be deficient in vitamins and minerals after being on the Quick Teenage Diet, but there are benefits in taking extra vitamins and minerals on any diet (and even in "normal" eating), at no time taking an excess of vitamin-mineral supplements.

If you cut down to eating very small amounts on QTD in order to lose pounds and trim off inches even more swiftly, then you may take a stronger "therapeutic" high-potency vitamin-mineral tablet once a day while on the diet.

■ BEVERAGES. It is desirable on QTD that you keep as much liquid as possible flowing through your system. Also, beverages before, during, after, and between meals help give you a satisfying feeling of "fullness" that helps replace a desire for food. You may drink all the artificially sweetened "no-calorie" flavored or plain soda you want, as often as you wish. By "no-calorie" beverages, I mean sodas and any drinks that contain no more than 1 calorie per ounce.

Don't drink any beverages containing sugar, or you'll be cutting down on the effectiveness of the diet in reducing you most quickly. Don't drink so-called "low-calorie" or "lower-in-calories" or "reduced calorie" beverages that contain more than 1 calorie per ounce. Read the label carefully, lest you drink dozens of calories per glassful and spoil the top efficiency of the quick-reducing process. Sodas made with sugar can contain between 85 to 130 calories per 8-oz. glass. A "part-sugar" glass of soda containing 48 calories is "lower-in-calories" than the regular sodas, but still too high in calories for swiftest QTD dieting.

Don't drink "fruit-flavored" drinks and powdered drinks made with sugar or part-sugar and therefore more than 1 calorie per ounce of beverage. An 8-oz. glass of canned fruit-flavored drink, orangeade, punch, and mixes containing sugar usually adds up to from 80 to 130 calories—much too much to help you slim swiftly, and providing your body with carbohydrates that interfere with the most efficient fat-burning functioning of the specific dynamic action of protein.

Don't drink tea mixes made with sugar. They add too many calories and carbohydrates to your daily intake for you to slim most rapidly as desired. Plain tea mixes to which you add artificial sweetening are fine on QTD.

Don't use any beverage additives made with sugar such as chocolate-flavored or other flavored syrups high in calories and carbohydrates. You may use "no-calorie" beverage flavorings, which are artificially sweetened and no more than 1 calorie per ounce of beverage.

You may drink coffee or tea if those beverages are already part of your daily eating, but without sugar, milk, or cream. You may use artificial sweeteners as desired. If you are a coffee drinker, take it black, or with just a dash of powdered non-dairy creamer or skim milk, if you must—but I prefer that you drink your coffee black, with or without artificial sweetening.

■ WATER. Drink an average of a half-glass of water per hour, as you see fit, not necessarily every hour on the hour. I want you to drink a total of at least eight 8-oz. glasses of water per day—and preferably more. That doesn't mean lining up 8 glasses of water at once and drinking them down. The total per day averages out to only a half-glass of water per waking hour—and certainly you can drink that small quantity of water, particularly when it's so great a help in taking off pounds and inches swiftly.

The water is necessary because this eating of practically all-protein foods burns up far more body fat than happens with most other diets. As a result, there are more waste products, or so-called "ashes" of burned fat. The drinking of water acts to wash out these waste products due to the burning up of your body fat in your system. This helps speed the reducing process and prevent any dryness or undesirable taste in the mouth, as the pounds "melt" from your body.

It may be of interest to know that on an all-protein diet, amino acids in the system are turned to urea, which must be washed out. Also, if there is too much uric acid in the blood, water washes it out effectively.

Drinking lots of water has many other health benefits, too. Water is helpful in beautifying the complexion, an aid in keeping the complexion clear. A sizable flow of water through your system helps to prevent constipation. During hot days, when the body loses much liquid through perspiration, drinking a good deal of water helps to keep you cooler and more comfortable.

A dentist writes that "water is the natural enemy of halitosis." He names "excessive fat in the diet" as one cause of bad breath, recommending, "don't pass the water faucet without taking a drink." The National Research Council for the Food and Drug Administration reported, "There is no convincing evidence that any medicated mouthwash, used as part of a daily hygiene regimen, has any therapeutic advantage over . . . water."

Keep in mind that "the noblest of the elements is water." As water helps to reduce you, it also aids your good health and energetic functioning in many other ways. Humans can survive for weeks without food when no food is available, but common elements you can't live

63

without for long include oxygen, water, and sleep. So consider drinking the half-glass of water per hour (totaling eight 8-oz. glasses a day) as a game, a benefit worth continuing for the rest of your life, even after you are slim and trim.

If you're at all concerned about being able to drink as many as 8 glasses of water a day, do this: Take a small 4-oz. orange juice glass and ask yourself, "Is it any problem to drink one small juice glass like that, filled with water, per hour?" Of course not. Well, that totals 8 glasses of water per day, it's a cinch.

YOUR BASIC-10 FOODS ON QTD

The foods and beverages described in the preceding material are the basic 10 from which you will choose what you want to eat at meals and at any other times of the day or evening. This gives you a wide variety of fine, satisfying foods and drinks that will help you take off pounds and inches with remarkable speed while keeping you healthful, vigorous, feeling good. Repeating the basic 10 in its briefest form:

> Skim milk: 1 or 2 glasses per day, depending on your age
> Lean meats: beef, lamb, or veal
> Chicken, turkey
> Lean fish
> Seafood
> Eggs
> Cottage cheese
> Vitamin-mineral tablet daily
> Beverages: "no-calorie" sodas, tea, coffee
> Water: eight 8-oz. glasses per day

In addition to the basic-10 foods and beverages, you may enjoy the following foods and flavorings on the Quick Teenage Diet:

> } Low-calorie, artificially sweetened gelatin
> }   dessert

You may enjoy a variety of flavors of low-calorie artificially sweetened gelatin dessert, made without sugar—up to 2 servings per day. Have this dessert at meals or between meals, whatever suits you best. Don't use any additives on the gelatin dessert—no fruits, toppings, whipped cream, or other whipped products, no sauces of any kind. Check the calorie content on the package and choose brands that are *no more than about 12 calories per serving.*

> } Consommé, bouillon, broth

You are permitted up to 3 cups per day of consommé, bouillon, or broth—homemade or made with cubes, powders, or liquids. Be sure that there is no fat in the brands you use, and no more than 10 calories per cup. The clear soups should be made from chicken, meat, or fish, but with no vegetable or fruit content in the making or serving. Enjoy a cup at meals or between meals, for evening snacks or whenever you wish—as another filling, satisfying item in your daily eating on QTD.

> } Ketchup, cocktail sauces

You may use these sauces *in very small amounts* just for flavoring, never heaping them on. Also, you may use very small amounts of mustard, chili sauce, pickle relish—but again, only a dash, never a sizable quantity. If you load up hamburgers, broiled frankfurters, or other per-mitted foods with sauces such as ketchup, mustard, and relish, you'll spoil the most efficient functioning of the specific dynamic action of protein to reduce you most speedily. Never use mayonnaise or any other creamy or oily sauces, no dressings, not even "low-calorie" mayon-naise or creamy salad dressings while on QTD.

꧁ Herbs, spices, seasonings

It's okay for you to use plain salt moderately, and also variations such as onion salt, celery salt, and garlic salt unless you are a water retainer (your doctor will have advised you of this in an examination), in which case you should use one of the brands of "salt substitute" available now.

You may use pepper, and common dried herbs and spices such as basil, bayberry, cinnamon, cloves, dill, garlic, marjoram, rosemary, thyme, and other herbs and seasonings to flavor eggs, meats, fish, poultry, anything permitted on the Quick Teenage Diet. However, use the seasonings, including salt and pepper, in moderation al-ways. Highly spiced servings are not recommended on this diet, nor on practically any diet. A few drops of fresh lemon juice are permitted on fish and other foods; a few drops of vanilla and other such flavorings are all right on cottage cheese, for example; *but never spoon on such flavoring additives.*

Make Up Your Own Daily Choices

A cartoon shows a doctor telling an unhappy over-weight, "On this diet, you eat all you want of everything you don't like." Fortunately you have many hearty, tasty foods you do like, a wide choice on the Quick Teenage Diet. You can select from this range of fine foods every day to make up your meals according to your own desires.

For example, for breakfast you might have scrambled eggs with a glass of milk or a cup of coffee (if you are a coffee drinker).

For lunch, you might have a cup of consommé, a lean broiled hamburger, a dish of low-calorie artificially sweetened raspberry gelatin dessert, and a beverage.

Your dinner could consist of a cup of chicken or beef broth, broiled chicken or steak or roast beef or lamb chop or baked halibut, topped off with a serving of low-calorie artificially sweetened orange gelatin dessert, and beverage of your choice.

For an evening snack, perhaps you'd choose to have a little creamed cottage cheese flavored with cinnamon and artificial sweetener, and a glass of artificially sweetened cream soda.

The choices are all up to you. Most teenagers on this diet find that it saves money over usual eating. While steak and roast beef sound expensive, there's no special high cost for chicken, fish, eggs, such comparatively lower-priced foods. Furthermore, while on the QTD diet, you save a good deal on the food budget by doing without costly cakes, cookies, ice cream, and other foods that you'd eaten plentifully before switching to the diet for the sake of your good looks and good health.

You'll find some helpful recipes in Chapter 12—and, like many other teenage dieters, you'll probably create additional recipes of your own.

To help you make your daily choices, several 7-Day Quick Teenage Diets are listed in Chapter 6. You need not follow any of my 7-day listings—they're given simply as guides. One of the reasons that QTD is so successful is that you satisfy your own desires from the list. You don't bother to count calories. There's no need for you to consult complicated lists for every meal and practically every hour of the day.

You simply choose from the following, given to you

here as a quick, convenient checklist (but be sure to read the detailed explanations and cautions given with each food category listing on the preceding pages).

Quick Teenage Diet Checklist

❭ Skim milk
❭ Lean meats
❭ Chicken, turkey
❭ Lean fish
❭ Seafood
❭ Eggs
❭ Cottage cheese
❭ Vitamin-mineral tablet daily
❭ Beverages
❭ Water
❭ Artificially sweetened gelatin dessert
❭ Consommé, bouillon, broth
❭ Ketchup, cocktail sauces
❭ Herbs, spices, seasonings

Important Guidelines

Eat all you want, but don't stuff yourself. This general guideline serves well for anyone who knows his or her normal limits. However, if you know that you are one of those persons who just keep shoving food in, then *limit yourself to small-to-moderate portions of the permitted foods—and stop right there.* Small-to-moderate portions of the all-protein foods, plus 1 or 2 glasses of skim milk that you'll drink each day, will take off those pounds and inches in a hurry, while keeping you healthful and energetic.

If you don't lose weight on QTD, you're cheating—knowingly or not. Check your daily eating carefully. The portions you're eating may be too large; if you take a large portion of meat or anything else, telling yourself that it's really a "moderate" or "small" amount, then you're only kidding yourself. For instance, you know the difference between an average-size lean hamburger and a big, double-size hamburger—yet if you eat double-size hamburgers you just won't be taking off pounds as rapidly.

If you are including such forbidden foods as fatty meats, chicken skin and fat, eggs fried in butter, a couple of slices of toast with jam, just "a few" cookies, a dish of ice cream, a chocolate soda, and so on, you're not following QTD, you're only fooling yourself. You'll be spoiling your "built-in will power," and the specific dynamic action of protein on QTD which makes your unwanted fat vanish amazingly. Shape up and follow the QTD listing of permitted foods and moderate portions accurately, if you want your figure to shape up beautifully. As a comedian said, "It's only good form to wear a bikini if you have a good form."

Choose a single food per "main dish," or combine foods. Your lunch might be 1 large frankfurter with a dash of mustard (never a mass of mustard), with a little pickle relish on the side, then a portion of artificially sweetened gelatin dessert, and a bottle of low-calorie artificially sweetened soda. Or, you might prefer to combine 1 small frankfurter and a little mustard on a dish with a couple of shrimps with a little cocktail sauce, and a little cottage cheese seasoned with herbs—then finish up with the low-calorie gelatin dessert and artificially sweetened soda. BUT—if you combined 2 frankfurters with a batch of shrimps and a mound of cottage cheese as your "main dish," you'd be overeating and stopping yourself from losing weight as rapidly as you'd really like.

Don't eat any foods not on the 14-point Quick Teenage Diet Checklist. That means *none* of the foods not included in that listing. No rich desserts . . . no soft drinks or milk concoctions containing sugar . . . no alcoholic drinks . . . and so on. If it's not in the listing, don't think that somebody has made a mistake of omission; *just don't eat it.* If you're doubtful about whether a food is permitted on QTD, and are about to eat it anyhow, ask yourself the question posed by Benjamin Franklin: "Who hath deceived thee so often as thyself?" Skip the forbidden food and you'll enjoy it more later on Keep-Slim Eating—after you're down to ideal weight and a beautiful slim, trim figure.

Don't eat any vegetables or fruits while on QTD. There's no question that vegetables and fruits are generally very "good for you," containing many nutritious elements. You can enjoy them plentifully after you are down to ideal weight and switch to Keep-Slim Eating. The reason for staying away from these fine foods is not calories alone, since vegetables are mostly low in calories—in fact, you can eat all the naturally low-calorie vegetables you'd want on an all-vegetable diet and never get fat (see Vegetables-Plus-Protein Diet later, if you especially like vegetables). The reason is simply that fruits and vegetables contain elements that would diminish the top efficiency of the QTD system of burning up extra body fat to slim you most rapidly.

While you're on the Quick Teenage Diet, don't eat any jams, jellies, preserves, or fruit toppings—except occasionally a little made with artificial sweetening. Again in this category, it is not a question of calories, but of unwanted carbohydrate contents. Don't eat any pickled cauliflower, corn, and so on.

Don't worry about missing vitamins on QTD—you don't! Your vitamin needs are taken care of if you follow my instructions and are in normal health (remember, I recommend checkup by a doctor before and after going on this or any diet). The proteins you are getting so plentifully provide all the vitamins and fat energy ordinarily needed by the human system.

For instance, you get vitamin C in the meat, fresh fish, and seafood that form part of the diet. The 1 or 2 glasses daily of skim milk supply other elements desirable in adolescence. In addition, you take a vitamin-mineral tablet every day as part of the diet.

I have seen teenagers lose as much as 100 pounds and more over a period of months on this diet—and none ever developed a clinical vitamin or mineral deficiency. QTD has *proved* with thousands upon thousands of teenagers that it takes off excess pounds and inches not only swiftly and surely, but also healthfully.

If you have been ill recently, or just recovered, ask your doctor if you can go on the Quick Teenage Diet (or any other diet). Keep in mind that the less excess fat your body has to carry, and your heart and other organs have to support, the better your chances for energetic good health. Overweight also tends to slow up recovery, and frequently leads to further sickness. You want to take excess fat and flab off as soon as possible, so check with your doctor.

If you "need" a snack because you think you feel hungry, don't eat anything not on the listing of permitted foods. You can select a snack from the listing easily; for instance . . . a bottle of artificially sweetened soda in your favorite flavor . . . a hard-boiled egg (or half an egg) sliced and sprinkled with herbs or other seasoning . . . a cup of chicken, beef, or fish bouillon (made in seconds with hot water and a cube or powder) . . . a little cottage cheese flavored with artificial sweetening and cinnamon, or other flavoring, or plain . . . a serving of artificially sweetened gelatin dessert in any flavor you like that's available . . . half a glass of skim milk (from your daily allotment), perhaps mixing in a little artificially sweetened flavoring . . . and so on.

Keep such snacks handy in the refrigerator. You're bright and creative, so choose or concoct your own snack from the full QTD listing.

If you have a sudden yen for something sweet, never reach for anything sugary or high-calorie. Remind yourself that such sweets spoil the swift-reducing process. Instead, drink down 1 or 2 glassfuls of satisfying, refreshing "no-calorie" artificially sweetened soda. Your "sweet tooth" can't tell the difference, but your slimmed-down figure will *show* the attractive difference.

Your appetite decreases on QTD. Instead of wanting more foods, you'll find that after a few days of this high-protein dieting your appetite diminishes and you eat less . . . naturally. Your eating habits and your taste preferences change. Many teenagers, after they get down to ideal weight, tell me that they "can't stand" very sweet or buttery, greasy foods—a great bonus in staying slim and healthier always.

You feel a great uplift of well-being usually after a few days on the Quick Teenage Diet. Many overweights, without even realizing it, suffer from a bloated, "heavy," sluggish feeling due to the many burdens of excess fat clogging the system. The day you start on QTD, the protein-fed "fires" begin burning excess fat out of your fat-storage pockets, and moving out unwanted waste matter rapidly.

A vital change will be taking place within you, physically and mentally, with your new way of eating and losing weight. There isn't much chance that you'll feel any undesirable effects at all, but if so, they're probably imaginary and due to the fact that you are depriving yourself of the foods and sweets that fattened you up in the first place. If your mouth feels dry, you're not drinking those 8 glasses of water each day (in addition to other permitted beverages).

If you should feel a bit sleepy or tired—you'll undoubtedly feel new energy, instead—sit or lie down for a brief rest, then get going actively again. If you feel very tired, again not likely, you may take 1 or 2 ounces of orange juice as a quick pickup. If you feel ill, which shouldn't happen because you're on the diet, switch to variety eating for a day or two, then go back on QTD—or check with your doctor. However, to repeat, it's highly unlikely that anything unsatisfactory will happen.

Lots more liquid will be moving through your system

than usual, which is excellent for your health and will also mean that you are urinating more often while you're on QTD. At the same time that a great deal of excess fats and waste are being removed from your body, you will also lose more water than usual as your weight and dimensions go down. Some people may try to tell you that you are losing water rather than fat, but this is not true. Actually the water is taking lots of fat along with it.

Understanding waste elimination is simple when you note that since the diet burns up fat swiftly, and you flush out much of it repeatedly with a flow of water and other liquids each day, there isn't much residue to eliminate. Therefore, if you don't have a bowel movement for a few days (or you may be as regular as ever), don't let it bother you. Keep in mind that nature soon makes adjustments, so that most individuals who usually have a bowel movement daily resume that schedule, in spite of the fact that residue is reduced naturally during the dieting period. But if you are at all concerned about a lack of daily bowel movement, take a little milk of magnesia as often as you think necessary.

If you have any natural allergy to any of the specific foods on the Quick Teenage Diet, such as some types of shellfish, perhaps, then substitute fresh fish or any of the other foods. In general, individuals tend to be much less allergic to the foods you are permitted on this diet than to sweets, oils, fats, and other rich foods that you will avoid.

If your cholesterol count is high—you will have been so informed by your doctor in checkup and other examinations, if that is the case—then eat a maximum of 4 eggs per week while on the diet or after you're at ideal weight. You are not permitted fats and other items that are naturally high in cholesterol, another benefit of this diet.

Artificially sweetened chewing gum may be eaten, but no more than 5 sticks a day. Check the labels, and don't use any sugarless gum that lists "carbohydrates" or "sorbitols" or "mannitols" or "hexitols." Don't eat any sugarless hard candies or soft candies, since they are likely to contain some carbohydrates and therefore interfere with the maximum efficiency of the QTD process of reducing you most quickly.

When eating in school lunchrooms or in restaurants, limit your eating only to items on the QTD list of permitted foods. In the school lunchroom, if choices are too few, bring along your lunch of a hard-boiled egg, a little cottage cheese, or a chicken leg with the skin removed, artificially sweetened gelatin dessert—there are lots of possibilities. Take along a bouillon cube or packet of powdered broth, get a cup of hot water, and make your own QTD clear soup. You can always get skim milk (or bring some in a Thermos bottle), or artificially sweetened sodas may be available.

Where there's a will, there's a way out of eating high-calorie or carbohydrate-content foods until you're slimmed to ideal weight. Even if you skip occasional lunches entirely, you'll lose nothing but excess fat. The rewards are worth the comparatively slight "sacrifices."

There's no real problem in restaurants, as hundreds of thousands of dieters testify who have reduced with the quick weight-loss methods. You can get practically anything you want by talking it over with the waiter; ask for what pleases you . . . lean broiled steak, hamburger or well-broiled frankfurter without the roll, shrimp and other seafood or fish or lean meats without butter or any sauces, and so on.

Millions of people in restaurants have ordered according to my rapid-reducing directions, and waiters are accustomed to providing just what is wanted. Your goal is *your ideal weight,* so let nothing swerve you from that target—you can achieve it without any question if you really want to.

Keep referring back to this book and keep rereading it to help keep you on the right track to quickest weight loss. You may wish to copy the listing of QTD permitted foods to carry in your purse or pocket—*but just the listing is not enough.* You must understand and keep reminding yourself of all the simple instructions, and the reasons for them. Because, no matter how many times you may have failed on other diets, you'll succeed in slimming down on this Quick Teenage Diet that works for you marvelously, with just a little cooperation on your part.

Keep on your toes physically as well as mentally, as I'll keep reminding you repeatedly. Don't pamper yourself physically at all—quite the opposite, keep moving, walking, working, be more active than ever. Don't lie around; avoid naps; don't sleep over 8 hours of each 24. Activity helps speed the slimming process in every way.

6-Meal QTD Dieting Subtracts MORE Pounds

If you want to lose even more weight, more rapidly than on normal QTD dieting as explained in this chapter, *spread the same food daily over 6 meals instead of the usual pattern of 3 meals per day.* The scientific explanation of this phenomenon is not quite clear, but it has been proved in repeated studies that 1,000 calories (or any set number) taken in 6 meals a day will reduce you more quickly than the same 1,000 calories eaten in 3 meals a day.

In fact, if you were not to eat any set meals, but instead spread the entire 1,000 calories of total daily eating by nibbling many times during the day, rather than at 3 or 6 "meals" per day, your weight loss would be even greater.

This is true with all-protein QTD eating, or with any variety of foods. The smaller the quantities eaten at a time—over 6 meals a day, rather than 3 meals a day—the quicker you'll lose weight. The human system apparently burns up smaller quantities of food spaced out in many feedings more quickly and efficiently, with less fat stored in the body, than the same amount of food eaten in the larger feedings three times a day.

If you prefer to lose weight more rapidly by "nibbling" instead of concentrating on the usual format of 3 meals a day, go to it. That's entirely up to you. The fact is that most of my overweight young people find it more desirable to continue the pattern of eating 3 meals a day as usual, but limiting the choice of foods according to the listing for the Quick Teenage Diet. Whichever way you do it, you'll slim down with QTD.

Don't ever overstuff with one huge meal, whether on the diet or on Keep-Slim Eating. This is very dangerous to your health. Studies of body chemistry show that a large, heavy meal has a far different effect in the system than a small feeding or snack. The body reacts to the big, heavy meal by pouring extra insulin into the blood. Insulin encourages the depositing of fat in the blood vessels and can bring on serious trouble.

Relax and have fun on the diet. For example, on her birthday, a QTD dieter with a sense of humor made for herself a miniature "birthday cake" of cottage cheese with colorful candles stuck in the top.

If you want super-speedy reducing results, you can try the Super-Quick Teenage Diets in the next chapter (Chapter 5). My entire purpose is to help you *get that weight off* in whatever way will work best for you. You make the choice according to your own make-up.

Your success will be my reward, as is the thrill I get every time I receive a letter like this one (from a newly slim teenage girl): "Dear Dr. Stillman . . . I have been on your diet for almost two months in preparation for my wedding in March. I bought a wedding dress two sizes too small, and am happy to say that the dress will most probably have to be taken in, as it fits almost perfectly now!!! Thank you so much for your marvelous ideas. I have tried many different diets, including starvation, eating fats, etc. Since I am a medical abstractor for a large organization, I have been used as a guinea pig for many regimes, running the gamut from pills to starvation, with very little success. I have now lost approximately 33 pounds (on your diet) ... THANK YOU SO MUCH!!!"

Don't Forget Your QTD Oxygen Exercise

To help increase your vital lung capacity, and to use up calories even faster, here's a repeat of the QTD Oxygen Exercise for your daily use:

Head up, shoulders back, lift your chest and pull in your stomach, breathe in (with mouth open slightly) for a slow count of 5, then expel the air. Repeat this slow breathing five times. That's all there is to it—it takes less than a minute.

Repeat this simple, pleasant "exercise" five or more times a day, whenever you think of it and it's convenient—sitting, standing, lying down. You'll feel better right after each time, and you'll speed up your reducing success.

5

The Super-Quick Teenage Diets

No two individuals are alike, nor do any persons burn up their food and excess fat at exactly the same rate. For most, the Quick Teenage Diet has been very successful in getting rid of extra pounds and inches rapidly.

However, some overweights, especially teenagers, are impatient to get that fat off in *super-quick* time, to trim off the inches almost overnight. If you are one of those who "just can't wait" to get rid of that ugly, unhealthy overweight, I can't blame you. Accordingly, for those impatient patients, I created two Super-Quick Teenage Diets. The "Regular" Super-Quick diet is for those who prefer a variety of all the high-protein foods on the QTD listing. The "Meat-Eater" Super-Quick Diet is for those who like meat particularly of the all-protein foods.

On these Super-Quick diets, many of the teenagers I have checked have lost 10 or more pounds a week. The diets are based on the same foods as the Quick Teenage Diet, but the difference is that while you still don't count calories, you *do* measure out the amounts of the protein foods you will eat each day. It's simple—only takes a minute or two for the whole day. You can weigh out the food once a day, or for each meal, as you see fit. Again, following my instructions, you run your daily dieting *yourself*.

Here are the actual amounts you figure out for yourself each day—the *maximum* amounts. You can eat less than these amounts if you wish, but not more per day:

SUPER-QUICK TEENAGE
DIET—REGULAR

4 oz. lean meat
5 oz. chicken or turkey
6 oz. fish or shellfish
2 eggs
4 oz. cottage cheese
1 8-oz. glass of skim milk (2 glasses if under 18)
I vitamin-mineral tablet
3 cups bouillon, consommé, or broth
2 portions artificially sweetened gelatin dessert
8 8-oz. glasses of water
all the coffee and tea you want (if you normally drink
  coffee and tea), without sugar, milk, or cream
all the "no-calorie" artificially sweetened soda you
  want, in a variety of flavors

SUPER-QUICK TEENAGE
DIET—MEAT-EATER

(These are *maximum* amounts permitted per day.)

8 oz. lean meat
4 oz. chicken or turkey
4 oz. fish or shellfish
1 egg
6 oz. cottage cheese
1 8-oz. glass of skim milk (2 glasses if under age 18)
I vitamin-mineral tablet
3 cups bouillon, consommé, or broth
2 portions artificially sweetened gelatin dessert
8 8-oz. glasses of water
all the coffee and tea you want (if you normally drink
  coffee and tea), without sugar, milk, or cream
all the "no-calorie" artificially sweetened soda you
  want, in a variety of flavors

Follow general Quick Teenage Diet instructions in the preceding chapter regarding the kinds of meats you may eat. Remove skin and fat from chicken and turkey. Use just a dash of mustard or ketchup, if any, and so on.

Eat 3 meals a day or more. You may divide up your daily amounts of food into 3 meals, or stretch it out into 5 or 6 feedings. You'll lose weight quicker in 5 or 6 feedings than in 3, as explained on earlier pages. *Allow at least 3 hours between feedings,* taking only beverages —as much as you want—between the feedings.

For example, if you wish to divide your daily diet allotment of food into 5 feedings, you might eat at 8 A.M. . . . 11 A.M. . . . 2 P.M. . . . 5 P.M. . . . 8 P.M. Or, of course, you may eat according to whatever is your accustomed schedule (the usual family meals) at perhaps 8 A.M. . . . noon . . . 6 P.M. The times for eating are your personal choice again, so long as you don't eat solid food for 3 hours or more between each meal.

Eat less, but not more. The Super-Quick diets don't take into account your age (except for drinking 1 glass of skim milk daily if age 18 or over, 2 glasses if under 18), or your height, since the food allotment is simplified to a general average. If you tend to be shorter in height than the average for your age, among your classmates or friends, eat *less* than the maximum given here.

You're eating few calories on these Super-Quick diets when based on my S.D.A. measurement (specific dynamic action of protein). Using normal calorie counts, both these diets total about 1,200 calories per day; however, according to my S.D.A. method of figuring, you are actually getting (compared with eating 1,200 calories in carbohydrate and variety foods) only about 650 to 850 calories per day in effect. That's why, eating these maximum quantities or less, the pounds drop swiftly on the scale day by day, and your body measurements trim down speedily.

You can lose up to 10 pounds and more in a week if you eat the maximum food listed for the two Super-Quick diets. In a typical instance, a teenage girl at age 18 had reduced to the point where she had a beautiful figure, was 5′ 7½″ tall, and weighed 127½ lbs.—ideal weight for her. She had become a model and was doing well at her profession. She came to me one day in a panic, since she said that she had a chance for a marvelous new modeling contract if she could lose 10 pounds within the next week, when she would report for the new job. Since the camera tends to make the body, arms, and legs look heavier, her employers required that she be even slimmer than her ideal weight (true also for many movie and TV actors and actresses, models, and beauty contest winners).

The young lady went on the Super-Quick Regular Teenage Diet. She told me that she made her portions a little smaller than listed for you . . . she skipped the skim milk . . . divided her food allotments into 5 feedings each day . . . walked a lot, and kept herself active.

Realize that it is much more difficult for a person to lose more pounds when at ideal weight than when very much overweight (I don't advise normally that you reduce below your ideal weight—my recommendation is that you attain your ideal weight and stay at that figure for your age and height). This young lady, with Super-Quick dieting as described, lost not 10 but *12 pounds in one week*. She showed up at the new job weighing 115½ pounds and photographed beautifully.

This lovely teenage model now maintains her weight at between 112 and 115 pounds. She looks exquisite and says she feels great. She is active, vigorous, works hard, and is brimming with health and vitality. She keeps her weight where she wants it by Keep-Slim Eating of a variety of foods. However, she reports that whenever she slips above the 115-pound mark on the scale, she goes back on the Quick Teenage Diet for a few days, and soon is right where she wants to be for her professional appearance.

This method of getting down to ideal weight, and staying there, is followed by many young men and young women. Some do it for professional reasons, but most, primarily, just to look and feel their best.

No "cheating." To attain the reducing success you want, you must not permit any deviation at all from the instructions for your Super-Quick dieting (or on QTD, for that matter). Eat only the amounts specified daily, or less if you wish to lose even faster. Don't stray to any of the foods prohibited on this form of high-protein eating—not a single cookie, not a spoonful of ice cream.

If you are tempted to slip, remind yourself that it's only a short time with Super-Quick dieting from thick to thin. Time enough to enjoy a forbidden sweet *after* you're down to your ideal weight and have switched to Keep-Slim Eating, but never *during* the dieting period.

Make up your own daily eating. From all the choices given to you on the Quick Teenage Diet listing, within the amounts specified for the Super-Quick diets, make your own selection. Here, just as one example out of loads of possibilities, is a typical daily menu that you might make up for yourself.

SUPER-QUICK TEENAGE DIET
DAY—REGULAR

Breakfast
  2 eggs boiled, or scrambled in no-fat pan
  1 8-oz. glass skim milk
  1 vitamin-mineral tablet
Mid-Morning Snack (or Mid-Afternoon)
  1 cup broth, seasoned to taste
Lunch
  1 cup chicken consommé
  5 oz. chicken or turkey

1 portion artificially sweetened gelatin dessert
Beverage
Dinner
1 cup beef bouillon
6 oz. shrimp cocktail (a dash of cocktail sauce)
4 oz. broiled steak, hamburger, or sliced lean meat
1 portion artificially sweetened gelatin dessert
Beverage
Evening Snack
2 oz. cottage cheese with artificial sweetening and cinnamon

~~~~~~~~~~~~~~~

During the day or evening, any time you wish, have coffee and tea (if you drink these normally), lots of "no-calorie" artificially sweetened sodas, and a "must"—eight 8-oz. glasses of water (spaced out half a glass an hour, or whenever you wish, so long as you drink at least 8 glasses per day).

~~~~~~~~~~~~~~~

If you're not losing weight rapidly, you are exceeding the size and/or amount of portions you should eat—whether on the Super-Quick diets or on the Quick Teenage Diet. Or, you may be snacking on "just a little" of foods that are not permitted, telling yourself that "such a little bit couldn't matter." It does matter—and as soon as you moderate your portions to what is recommended, or *less* if you want to drop pounds and inches more speedily, you'll lose weight wonderfully.

If you slip off the Super-Quick or QTD diets, don't waste time moaning about it. There's absolutely no sense in crying over swilled calories. There's no profit in punishing yourself with remorse. Just start right in again on the Super-Quick diet, and you'll soon be losing pounds super-speedily.

6

The 7-Day Quick Teenage Diet

A popular overweight TV comedian often pats his bulging stomach and delivers the joke, "I went on a 7-day diet . . . and all I lost was a week!" Unfortunately that happens on too many diets that aim to taper you off slowly and gradually instead of taking off 5 or more pounds quickly and dramatically in seven days.

When you see the pounds and inches disappearing in a hurry, that's when you're convinced that you're on the way to the slimness you want. The 7-Day Quick Teenage Diet in this chapter is designed to reduce you swiftly, thus proving to you that becoming slim and trim is not a dream, but a goal within your reach. You just follow this simple, clear reducing method for a relatively short time.

You *will* lose 5, 10, or more pounds in seven days (depending on how overweight you are); you *will* take off 5 percent to 10 percent of your weight—if you follow the diet exactly. You must stay with small-to-moderate portions, limit yourself to the foods on the Quick Teenage Diet as given in detail previously, and not cheat at all. As a result, within seven days you'll see a big drop in weight and a significant loss of inches that will delight you. (If you don't lose, you're doing something wrong—and usually know that you're fooling yourself one way or another.)

Then you continue on this 7-Day Quick Teenage Diet for another week, and another, if necessary. After a few weeks, you will have lost a lot of weight, but if you still are not at your ideal weight, you may wish to take a break for a week and go on Keep-Slim Eating, with a variety of foods, counting calories. After a week of change, go back on the 7-Day Quick Teenage Diet until you're at your desired weight.

Important: Most teenagers, in reducing on my Quick Teenage Diet, prefer to make up their own menus each day, selecting from the permitted foods listed earlier. However, I find that some overweights like to have the diet spelled out for them day by day. If that's what you wish, then the 7-Day Quick Teenage Diet can be your personal best way to swift, certain reducing.

Follow All the Simple Guidelines

The entire Quick Teenage Diet is spelled out for you in Chapter 4. Reread that chapter, and go on the 7-Day QTD listed here if you prefer that to selecting your own foods. Be sure to drink the 8 glasses of water per day . . . enjoy the "no-calorie" artificially sweetened sodas in a variety of flavors . . . coffee and tea if they're part of your normal eating . . . and all the other suggestions that make up effective QTD reducing. Get plenty of activity and exercise, and remember to do the deep-breathing QTD Oxygen Exercise five to six times daily

You will get the quick-reducing benefits of the specific dynamic action of protein every day on the 7-Day Quick Teenage Diet. As explained, and as any physiologist can affirm, this kind of practically all-protein eating burns up foods in the system 18 percent to 50 percent more effectively than with a "balanced diet" of a variety of different types of foods. Protein is also more filling than other elements, and as you proceed day after day on this diet, your appetite diminishes instead of increasing.

Day by day on this 7-day diet, the protein-eating is burning up fat more quickly and efficiently. It is pulling more fat out of the fat-storage depots in your body, and stopping the accumulation of fat depots in your system more effectively. The protein cannot be deposited—rather, it is readily excreted by your system. You are avoiding foods with sugars and carbohydrates that turn to fat, and in turn are deposited as fat.

With the week of QTD protein-eating, you'll find that you're looking and feeling better day by day. As fat deposits are stopped, and fats are pulled out of the depots and eliminated, swelling and bloating from overeating and overweight are diminished and even eliminated.

And, so vital, during this week of QTD protein-eating, you get a complete, not just a partial break, from your past eating habits that made you fat. This complete change of eating works, whereas simply eating smaller portions of the same foods in general fails dishearteningly for most teenage overweights.

Diet one day at a time. As the days go by, your weight will go down, and so will your appetite. You will have finished the week almost before you know it, wonderfully slimmer by pounds. You may have read the line from Cicero: "One day well spent is to be preferred to an eternity of error." Each day on the 7-Day Quick Teenage Diet will help take you away from a lifetime, a seeming eternity, of being overweight.

Mix and Match As You Please

You may follow the 7-Day QTD listing exactly, or substitute your own selections wherever you like—as long as you stay within the basic Quick Teenage Diet listing. For example, on the Monday listing, if you prefer hamburger to frankfurter for lunch, just make the switch. If roast lamb or chicken or broiled fish or steak is being served for the family dinner, it's okay to have a moderate portion of one of those instead of the roast beef listed. If you prefer your skim milk at dinner or mid-afternoon instead of at breakfast or lunch, that's fine. Suit yourself to slim yourself.

You may shuffle meals—lunch for breakfast, dinner for lunch—however you see fit and feel that day. Or, you may wish to switch days—Thursday's meals instead of Monday's, Wednesday's dinner instead of Tuesday's dinner—as you choose. Don't hesitate to change dishes or recipes, such as seasoning cottage cheese as you like that day instead of as listed. Even make up your own recipes, as long as the ingredients are permitted on QTD eating. Substitute farmer cheese or pot cheese for creamed cottage cheese if you'd prefer that change—the decision is yours, just as the weight loss is all your own.

If you want a snack in mid-morning, afternoon, or evening—even though it's not listed—go ahead and enjoy something. Just make sure that you choose one of the permitted items, such as broth, consommé, or bouillon . . . cottage cheese . . . artificially sweetened gelatin dessert . . . a hard-boiled egg . . . "no-calorie" artificially sweetened soda in your favorite flavors . . . coffee or tea, if part of your regular eating . . . and so on, checking with the basic QTD listing.

Your beverage can be any flavor of "no-calorie" artificially sweetened soda . . . coffee or tea (without sugar, milk, or cream), if part of your normal eating . . . 1 or 2 glasses of skim milk daily (2 glasses if under 18 years old, 1 glass if aged 18 or over).

If you lunch in school, choose items that are on the 7-Day QTD listing, if available. Unfortunately, most meals served in school lunchrooms are high in calories and starch—foods such as macaroni and cheese, meat loaf with bread fillers and served with french-fried potatoes or mashed potatoes or rice drenched in heavy gravies. *Avoid such foods completely!* Bring your own lunch—a container of broth, a hard-boiled egg and some cottage cheese, a container of artificially sweetened gelatin dessert, and your beverage, or get the skim milk or "no-calorie" drink in the lunchroom.

Don't ever be concerned that you may be eating "differently" from others at school. You know where you're going—you're on the road to a slimmer, healthier figure. The joy of achieving that will overbalance by far any possible embarrassment about being "different" by bringing food and eating exactly as you have determined to on QTD. As Longfellow put it: "He that respects himself is safe from others; he wears a coat of mail that none can pierce." You gain increased self-respect with every ounce you lose.

Start your 7-Day Quick Teenage Diet—and see the remarkable weight loss difference by the end of the week.

7-DAY QUICK TEENAGE DIET

MONDAY

Breakfast
    1 vitamin-mineral tablet
    1 scrambled egg with herbs
    Small portion cottage cheese
    1 glass skim milk
Lunch
    1 cup chicken bouillon
    1 frankfurter with dash of mustard and a little pickle relish
    Artificially sweetened gelatin dessert
    Beverage
    1 glass skim milk (if under age 18)
Dinner
    3 medium-size shrimps with a little cocktail sauce
    Moderate portion roast beef (or other lean meat)
    Small portion cottage cheese, seasoned if desired
    Artificially sweetened gelatin dessert
    Beverage

TUESDAY

Breakfast
    1 vitamin-mineral tablet

1 sunny-side-up egg (fried in no-fat pan)
Small portion cottage cheese with cinnamon and artificial sweetening
1 glass skim milk

Lunch
1 cup beef broth
Medium-size broiled hamburger with dash of ketchup
Artificially sweetened gelatin dessert
Beverage
1 glass skim milk (if under 18)

Dinner
1 cup clear fish broth
Broiled scallops with a little chili sauce if wanted
Medium portion cottage cheese mixed with minced clams and herbs
Artificially sweetened gelatin dessert
Beverage

WEDNESDAY

Breakfast
1 vitamin-mineral tablet
2-egg omelet with herbs
1 glass skim milk

Lunch
1 cup clear broth
Medium-size lean cube steak (trim off fat)
Small portion seasoned cottage cheese
Artificially sweetened gelatin dessert
Beverage
1 glass skim milk (if under age 18)

Dinner
Small crabmeat cocktail with a little cocktail sauce
1 broiled lean lamb chop (trim off all visible fat)
Small portion cottage cheese, seasoned to taste
Artificially sweetened gelatin dessert
Beverage

Breakfast

    1 vitamin-mineral tablet

    2 boiled eggs

    1 glass skim milk

Lunch

    1 cup chicken consommé

    1 chicken leg (skin removed)

    Small portion cottage cheese

    Artificially sweetened gelatin dessert

    Beverage

    1 glass skim milk (if under age 18)

Dinner

    Small portion drained salmon with drops of fresh lemon juice

    Lean roast lamb (remove all visible fat)

    Small portion cottage cheese with herbs

    Artificially sweetened gelatin dessert

    Beverage

Breakfast

    1 vitamin-mineral tablet

    1-egg omelet made with bits of drained salmon

    1 glass skim milk

Lunch

    1 cup fish broth

    Lean chicken slices (or leg or thigh)

    Small portion cottage cheese, mixed with a little ketchup if desired

    Artificially sweetened gelatin dessert

    Beverage

    1 glass skim milk (if under age 18)

Dinner

    3 medium-size shrimps with a little cocktail sauce

    Moderate portion broiled salmon steak with herbs

    Small portion cottage cheese, seasoned as desired

Artificially sweetened gelatin dessert
Beverage

Breakfast
1 vitamin-mineral tablet
Scrambled egg made with bits of all-beef bologna
1 glass skim milk
Lunch
1 cup turkey broth (no fat)
½ turkey leg
Small portion cottage cheese seasoned with herbs
Artificially sweetened gelatin dessert
Beverage
1 glass skim milk (if under age 18)
Dinner
Small portion water-packed tuna with drops of fresh
 lemon juice
Medium-size portion broiled steak (trim off all visible
 fat)
Small portion cottage cheese mixed with a little chili
 sauce if desired
Artificially sweetened gelatin dessert
Beverage

Breakfast
1 vitamin-mineral tablet
1 scrambled egg with bits of broiled, drained frankfurter
1 glass skim milk
Lunch
1 cup beef bouillon
Moderate portion drained salmon with drops of fresh
 lemon juice
Small portion cottage cheese with herbs
Artificially sweetened gelatin dessert

Beverage
1 glass skim milk (if under age 18)
Dinner
   3 medium-size shrimps with a little cocktail sauce
   Moderate portion sliced roast turkey (or leg or thigh)
   Small portion seasoned cottage cheese
   Artificially sweetened gelatin dessert
   Beverage

Feel Elated, Not Deprived

All the time that you're on the 7-Day Quick Teenage Diet (and if you're on for repeated weeks necessarily, depending on how overweight you are to start), feel happy and excited by the wonderful results you're going to see within the week, then a second week, and perhaps another, if needed. Don't ever let yourself feel deprived—nor permit anyone else to give you that false idea. Rather, you're privileged to be on your way to accomplishing something important and lasting for yourself.

Being healthier, slim and more attractive, more limber and graceful, enjoying the free movement of your trim, compact body—that's worth a thousand times more than anything obtained from stuffing your stomach. "Life is an ecstasy," Emerson said—but not when your body and spirit are overwhelmed by the constant burden of excess fat and flab.

Keep in mind, if you ever hesitate on the diet, that a relatively short period of QTD reducing will bring you to your goal of ideal weight and slim attractiveness.

Why You Will Lose Weight Now and Keep Slim

If you have any doubt at all that this proved reducing method will work for you, take a few seconds to read this typical letter from an extremely attractive young woman (who included her snapshot). She wrote: ". . . I am so anxious to tell you of my success with your diet. . . I am 18 years old and will graduate from high school next month. I have been a 4-year honor student and I am Valedictorian of my class. . . This weekend my class is putting on a play in which I have a leading role. . .

"All my life I have had a weight problem. . . When I was a high school freshman I gained weight until I reached a peak of 152 pounds. I am 5′ 5″ tall. . . I just kept gaining until I weighed 168 lbs. Isn't that terrible? . . . I was really desperate, so I decided that I would try your diet for one week and see what happened. The first week I lost 9 pounds and was I thrilled. . . Your diet is really wonderful. My stomach never growls and I never feel weak. I have more energy now than I have had for a long time. Since the beginning of my diet I have lost 21 pounds. I feel great. . .

"Gee, Dr. Stillman, you are a life-saver. I would like to thank you from the bottom of my heart for your wonderful diet. I am an old hand with diets, and pills, and feeling hungry, and I think that your diet is the best plan I have ever tried, and I would recommend it to anyone who has had a lot of trouble losing weight like me. . . I actually enjoy being on your diet, it is so rewarding to be on a diet and really lose weight."

This bright teenager goes on to say that she knows now that she can finally reach her ideal weight. The key points you should note are, first, her statement that *"I decided that I would try your diet for one week and see what happened."* Second, check her comment that "it is so rewarding to be on a diet and really lose weight." She lost 9 pounds her first week. Then she went on to drop 21 pounds, and more, as you can.

Furthermore, any time you put on a few pounds over your desired weight, you can go right back on one of these rapid-reducing diets—and be slim and trim again in several days. You can count on that help for the rest of your life.

Try this 7-Day Quick Teenage Diet for one short week, repeat as often as necessary (or switch to any of the other speedy-reducing diets in this book, if you wish). Use it as a handy quick-reducing method always. Once you learn the QTD way to slimming success, you'll never again be "a poor loser."

7

The Quick Teenage Dividend Diet

"DIVIDEND: anything received as a bonus, reward, or in addition to or beyond what is expected." (Dictionary.)

Among the thousands of teenagers who have lost weight with these high-protein speedy-reducing methods, some have asked, "Please, Dr. Stillman, can't I have a slice of bread—just one slice of bread a day for the change?" Others have requested a vegetable or a favorite fruit, ice cream or cookies or cake. I tried this with some of my teenage overweights and found that while they didn't do well on "fat dividends" such as financial investors want, they lose weight well on the "skinny dividends" we worked out together.

So, for those of you who may think occasionally, like the poet William Cowper, that "variety's the very spice of life, that gives it all its flavour," I've provided for you in the Quick Teenage Dividend Diet a special "dividend" of one food that isn't all protein—each day. On this diet you won't lose pounds quite as rapidly as with the regular Quick Teenage Diet listed earlier. However, if you allow yourself just one dividend per day as spelled out in the following, in a small-to-moderate portion, you'll lose weight surely and satisfactorily. It may be just the ticket for you personally to *get that weight off*.

Choose Your Own Dividend

You can select for yourself one (and only one) of these items per day:

* 1 slice of bread (or small roll)
* 1 cup of low-calorie vegetables such as asparagus, carrots, lettuce, spinach, tomatoes (see list of low-calorie vegetables in chapter on Keep-Slim Eating) . . . hot or cold, or as a salad, as you prefer
* a low-calorie fruit such as a medium-size apple or orange, or a half grapefruit, whatever you personally choose
* a small portion of ice cream or ice milk, your favorite flavor
* a small wedge of plain cake, or 2 medium-size plain cookies

If you prefer, you may have the same dividend every day, a slice of bread, a vegetable or fruit, or whatever you want most—*but only one dividend per day.* You will lose weight more quickly if you do without the dividend and stay with the protein foods, as noted before. But . . . you should still lose pounds per week on this high-protein dividend diet.

The 7-Day Teenage Dividend Diet listing that follows is designed to serve as a guide for you so that you can make up your own day's eating from the permitted foods you like best. For example, instead of Monday's breakfast of a sliced small orange (the day's dividend), a boiled egg, and the skim milk, you might prefer 2 poached eggs and skim milk and a hot beverage—suit yourself. If you want the listed snacks with your meals, it's up to you. The goal is the same: to get those unhealthy, unattractive extra pounds off quickly, surely, safely.

7-DAY TEENAGE DIVIDEND DIET

MONDAY . . . Fruit Dividend*

Breakfast
 *1 small orange, sliced
 1 boiled egg
 1 glass skim milk
 Coffee or tea if desired, and if you drink them normally
Mid-Morning Snack
 1 cup of chicken bouillon
Lunch
 1 cup of clear beef broth
 1 medium-size broiled hamburger with a little ketchup
 Small portion cottage cheese mixed with dill
 Beverage
 1 glass skim milk (if you are under age 18)
Mid-Afternoon Snack
 Artificially sweetened gelatin dessert
Dinner
 3 medium shrimps with a little cocktail sauce
 Medium-size broiled steak (trim off all fat)
 Small portion cottage cheese, seasoned to taste
 Beverage
Evening Snack
 Cup of broth, or artificially sweetened gelatin dessert

TUESDAY . . . Bread Dividend*

Breakfast
 *1 slice toast with artificially sweetened jelly
 Small portion cottage cheese
 1 glass skim milk
 Coffee or tea if desired
Mid-Morning Snack
 Cup of beef bouillon
Lunch
 1 cup of chicken consommé

2 broiled or boiled all-beef frankfurters with a little
   mustard
Beverage
1 glass skim milk (if you are under age 18)
Mid-Afternoon Snack
Artificially sweetened gelatin dessert
Dinner
1 cup of fish broth
Broiled salmon steak with a little pickle relish
Small portion cottage cheese with herbs
Beverage
Evening Snack
Cup of broth, or artificially sweetened gelatin dessert

WEDNESDAY . . . Vegetable Dividend*
Breakfast
1 egg scrambled in no-fat pan
Small portion cottage cheese
1 glass skim milk
Coffee or tea if desired
Mid-Morning Snack
1 cup of chicken broth
Lunch
Broiled halibut
*Medium portion asparagus with herbs
Beverage
1 glass skim milk (if you are under age 18)
Mid-Afternoon Snack
Artificially sweetened gelatin dessert
Dinner
Shrimp cocktail (3 medium-size shrimps with a little
   cocktail sauce)
Lean roast lamb, with a little pickle relish if wanted
Small portion cottage cheese, seasoned to taste
Beverage
Evening Snack
Cottage cheese with cinnamon and artificial sweetening

100

THURSDAY . . . Ice Cream Dividend*

Breakfast
  2 sunny-side-up eggs
  1 glass skim milk
  Coffee or tea if desired

Mid-Morning Snack
  1 cup of beef bouillon

Lunch
  1 cup of fish broth
  Canned salmon, rinsed in water and drained, with
    drops of fresh lemon juice
  Cottage cheese mixed with a little pickle relish
  Beverage
  1 glass skim milk (if you are under 18)

Mid-Afternoon Snack
  Artificially sweetened gelatin dessert

Dinner
  1 cup of chicken consommé
  Roast chicken with skin removed
  Small portion of cottage cheese mixed with chives
  *Small portion ice cream or ice milk (fewer calories)
  Beverage

Evening Snack
  1 cup of broth or artificially sweetened gelatin dessert

FRIDAY . . . Salad Dividend*

Breakfast
  1 hard-boiled egg
  Small portion cottage cheese mixed with a little arti-
    ficially sweetened jelly, if desired
  1 glass skim milk
  Coffee or tea if desired

Mid-Morning Snack
  1 cup of chicken bouillon

Lunch
  1 cup beef broth

1 lean small turkey leg

Small portion cottage cheese mixed with your favorite dried herbs

Beverage

1 glass skim milk (if you are under age 18)

Mid-Afternoon Snack

Artificially sweetened gelatin dessert

Dinner

3 medium-size shrimps (or crabmeat) with a little cocktail sauce

Moderate portion of lean roast beef (trim off all visible fat)

*Small lettuce and tomato salad with a little fresh lemon juice

Beverage

Evening Snack

Cottage cheese with orange extract flavoring, artificial sweetening

SATURDAY ... Cake Dividend*

Breakfast

2 eggs scrambled in no-fat pan

Small portion artificially sweetened jam

1 glass skim milk

Coffee or tea if desired

Mid-Morning Snack

1 cup of beef bouillon

Lunch

1 cup fish broth

Tuna fish, water-packed or drained, with a little pickle relish

Beverage

1 glass skim milk (if you are under age 18)

Mid-Afternoon Snack

Artificially sweetened gelatin dessert

Dinner

Shrimp cocktail with cocktail sauce
Medium-size broiled steak (trim off all fat)
Small portion cottage cheese with herbs
*Small slice plain cake, or 2 medium-size plain cookies
Beverage

Evening Snack
Artificially sweetened gelatin dessert

SUNDAY . . . Ice Milk Dividend*

Breakfast
1-egg omelet made with 1 slice broiled, drained all-
  beef bologna
1 glass skim milk
Coffee or tea if desired

Mid-Morning Snack
1 cup of chicken bouillon

Lunch
Small crabmeat cocktail with a little cocktail sauce
Broiled lean lamb chop with a little pickle relish
Small portion cottage cheese, seasoned to taste
Beverage
1 glass skim milk (if you are under age 18)

Mid-Afternoon Snack
Artificially sweetened gelatin dessert

Dinner
1 cup beef bouillon
Roast chicken leg, thigh, or slices
Small portion cottage cheese mixed with minced chives
  or onion flakes
*Small portion ice milk, your favorite flavor
Beverage

Evening Snack
Cottage cheese mixed with nutmeg and artificial sweetening

Make no mistake about it, in one week on this diet you will lose 5 percent or more of your weight, a total of 5 or more pounds. If you don't, then you're doing something wrong—you're fooling yourself by adding forbidden foods, or you may be eating such oversize portions and quantities that you don't lose enough, or you are helping yourself to excessive portions of the dividend foods.

Don't overeat, or you'll just be kidding yourself. These high-protein foods are more filling than others, and small-to-moderate portions will be satisfying. Don't stuff yourself with more calories than your system can burn up properly for desired weight loss. Don't eat any foods not listed for the regular Quick Teenage Diet; if you have any doubts about whether or not a food is permitted, don't eat it.

Don't forget 8 glasses of water per day, plus lots of "no-calorie" beverages, coffee and tea as desired, and the 1 or 2 glasses of skim milk daily. Also, remember your daily vitamin-mineral tablet.

You won't be hungry eating fine, filling meats, fish, and the other all-protein foods permitted. Remember, you don't have to eat everything listed on this 7-Day Dividend Diet—the smaller the amounts you eat, the more unwanted fat you'll lose. Skip anything you don't want.

Get your doctor's approval (as I point out repeatedly) before you go on this or any diet. This diet, although thoroughly healthful, is not for teenagers with any medical problem, nor for a pregnant woman. That applies to any restricted reducing diet, no matter how effective.

You will succeed in losing pounds and inches when you follow this Dividend Diet just as directed. It's not quite as speedy as QTD reducing, but as long as it works for you, that's our mutual goal. After a week, if you're still overweight, continue for another week, and another, until you're as beautifully slim as you aim to be. After a few weeks of this dieting, take a week's change on Keep-Slim Eating of a variety of foods, counting calories so you don't gain weight. Then, after a week, go back on the regular Quick Teenage Diet or the Dividend Diet.

Use the QTD Oxygen Exercise (see Chapter 1) on this Dividend Diet and as long as you are overweight. (That deep-breathing exercise is excellent also for you or anyone at any weight, and worth keeping up daily for the rest of your life.)

8

Other Teenage Diets to Drop Pounds Quickly

Every reducing diet in this book is a speedy-weight-loss diet, to take pounds and inches off your body in a hurry. I can't repeat this basic point too often: The reason is that losing a *number* of pounds a week—not just 1 or 2 pounds in seven days with the usual "balanced" diets—provides the "built-in will power" to keep you dieting and losing weight.

A bestseller book, show, and movie had the title, *How to Succeed . . . Without Really Trying*. Diets that are slow, trimming off about a pound a week (or nothing, when the dieter gives up) might be titled, "How to Try Without Really Succeeding." That won't happen with any reducing diet I ever recommend. You can count on losing plenty of pounds and inches on any of these diets because they all have been *proved successful*. My standard for any diet I recommend (whether I created it, or any other dieting method) can be summed up in two words: *it works*—quickly, effectively, healthfully.

My finding through the years has been that the most successful reducing diet for teenagers is the Quick Teenage Diet. It consists of practically all-protein foods, and is based on SDA, the specific dynamic action of protein in burning up fat most efficiently, as previously explained. The diets in this chapter are not all-protein, but are keyed to a variety of foods for that smaller percentage of those individuals who need a range of foods in order to keep dieting and reducing.

My chief concern is in helping "the shape of things"—females and males. Therefore, I'm not fenced in by any rigid rules or theories about the "proper" way to reduce. My total aim is to help you *get that weight off* healthfully, and keep it off. If variety is your cup of tea (without cream and sugar, of course), then try one or more of these speedy-reducing variety diets to slim down rapidly, surely.

Change Diets Weekly if You Wish

You might go on the Quick Teenage Diet one week, switch to one of the variety diets the next week, back to the Quick Teenage Diet the third week (if you are still overweight), on to a different variety diet the following week, and so on. You'll be losing weight happily each week because, although you won't be counting calories (they'll be counted for you beforehand in most cases), your daily calorie consumption will be low if you follow each diet exactly as instructed—and *you'll lose weight quickly.*

7-DAY QUICK VARIETY DIETS

In the three diets that follow, I've scheduled for you in detail a full week of meals—since some individuals reduce well with these day-by-day instructions. Take it one day at a time. When you're dieting on Monday, then concentrate just on that one day—let Tuesday take care of itself, as you take care of Tuesday's dieting tomorrow.

You don't count calories for yourself on these 7-Day diets, as I've taken care of the calorie-counting for you. The calories average out to about 500-600 calories per day—so you'll be losing weight rapidly. You should drop 5 pounds or more per week, depending on how overweight you are, losing at least 5 percent, probably more, of your total weight in the first week alone. But don't deviate—when you turn to your diet every day, don't make any U-turns.

A switch you can make is to shift around days and comparable meals, if you wish. For instance, you can repeat Tuesday's meals on Wednesday if you wish, or substitute any day for another. You can switch one day's lunch, or breakfast, or dinner, for another day's listing for lunch, or breakfast, or dinner. In such switching, the total number of calories per day will remain about the same.

Abide faithfully day after day on the diets, and you'll find that instead of having an increased desire for food, your appetite decreases. You get along pleasantly on less. Before you know it, the week is over, and you are pounds lighter and more attractive. Friends will start remarking about how much slimmer and better you look. You'll find, too, that you feel healthier, more vigorous and alive, as the burdensome fat melts away. Instead of being weaker from the weight loss, you'll feel stronger, like the "new person" you want to be.

7-Day Diets Checklist

1. Take 1 vitamin-mineral pill a day while on any of the 7-day diets.

2. Drink lots of water and other beverages all during your waking hours. Drink at least 6 8-oz. glasses of water in each 24 hours, plus plenty of "no-calorie" artificially sweetened sodas, 1 to 2 glasses of skim milk per day (2 glasses per day if you're under age 18), as much as you want of coffee and tea if you drink them normally—but without sugar, milk, or cream (it's okay to add a dash of skim milk or non-dairy powdered creamer, and artificial sweetening, if you wish).

The more liquid you drink the better, since you are burning up fat more rapidly than usual on this very low-calorie eating. The flow of liquids helps wash out the waste matter that is leaving your fat deposits every day that you're dieting. As the unhealthy excess fat is being pulled out of the fat-storage depots in your body, the liquids help remove it swiftly from your system.

3. *You may enjoy some low-calorie snacks* during the day and evening if you wish, as long as you don't overdo it. Choose from the following:

. . . Portion of artificially sweetened gelatin dessert (no more than 12 calories per portion).

. . . Cup of clear broth, consommé, or bouillon, made from cubes, powder, or liquid concentrate—or other clear soups from which all fats have been removed.

. . . 2 to 3 raw carrot strips.

. . . 2 or 3 cucumber strips.

. . . 1 or 2 stalks of raw celery.

. . . some fresh lettuce leaves.

4. *Don't use any butter,* margarine, fats, oils, or regular dressings on vegetables, salads, or on other foods. You may use a little low-calorie dressing on salads.

5. *Don't use any fats in cooking.* Keep in mind that the longer you broil, bake, or simmer meats, fish, and poultry, the more readily they are digested thoroughly, and the same portion has fewer calories, another aid in reducing.

6. *Cut all your food in small pieces,* and eat slowly, chewing and stretching out the portion for a longer time.

7. *Keep active*—walking, bicycling, swimming, exercising, engaging in sports that keep your body in motion as much as possible.

8. *Use the QTD Oxygen Exercise* five to six times a day (see instructions in Chapter 1) to improve your deep breathing and lung capacity in order to use up calories more efficiently and quickly.

9. *DON'T stray from the diet listings.* Don't add foods, pile in extras, or increase portions permitted. Keep dieting just one short week—and see the wonderful slimming difference. If you do fall off a day, don't waste time and energy weeping about the failure. Instead, go right back on the diet and make it a fat-smashing success!

MONDAY

Breakfast

    1 vitamin-mineral tablet

    1 egg poached, boiled, scrambled or fried in a no-fat pan

    I slice of extra-thin toast with artificially sweetened jam or jelly if desired

    1 glass skim milk

Lunch

    1 cup of low-calorie bouillon, broth, or consommé

    Salad of 1 sliced hard-boiled egg on 5 or 6 lettuce leaves, with low-calorie salad dressing

    Beverage

Dinner

    6 ounces of broiled fish with fresh lemon juice and herbs and spices (no butter or margarine)

    1 broiled tomato

    ½ cup spinach or other vegetable

    1 serving of artificially sweetened gelatin dessert

    Beverage

Extra Snack

    ½ medium-size apple

TUESDAY

Breakfast

    1 vitamin-mineral tablet

    1 sliced orange

    2 tablespoons of cottage cheese

    1 glass skim milk

Lunch

    1 cup of bouillon, broth, or consommé

    Hot vegetable plate of 1 cup each of 3 low-calorie vegetables

    Beverage

Dinner
- 1 cup of bouillon, broth, or consommé
- 4 ounces of broiled, lean hamburger
- Salad of ½ sliced tomato on generous serving of lettuce, seasoned with fresh lemon juice and herbs and spices, or low-calorie salad dressing if desired
- 1 serving of artificially sweetened gelatin dessert
- Beverage

Extra Snack
- ½ grapefruit, with artificial sweetening if preferred

WEDNESDAY

Breakfast
- 1 vitamin-mineral tablet
- 1 egg boiled, or scrambled or fried in no-fat pan
- 1 slice of extra-thin toast with artificially sweetened jam or jelly if desired
- 1 glass skim milk

Lunch
- 1 cup of low-calorie bouillon, broth, or consommé
- 1 all-beef frankfurter split and broiled, with mustard and a little pickle relish if wanted
- Wedge of lettuce, good-sized, with low-calorie salad dressing if desired
- Beverage

Dinner
- 1 cup of bouillon, broth, or consommé
- 5 ounces of broiled chicken (skin removed)
- 1 half-cup each of 2 favorite low-calorie vegetables (choice of asparagus, carrots, green beans, spinach, broccoli, cauliflower, tomatoes)
- 1 serving of artificially sweetened gelatin dessert
- Beverage

Extra Snack
- ½ cup of artificially sweetened or natural apple sauce, when wanted

Breakfast

   1 vitamin-mineral tablet

   ½ sliced orange

   1 slice of extra-thin toast with artificially sweetened jam or jelly if desired

   1 glass skim milk

Lunch

   1 cup of bouillon, broth, or consommé

   1 medium-size tomato stuffed with crabmeat, on lettuce leaves

   1 carrot, shredded

   Beverage

Dinner

   1 cup of vegetable soup, including the vegetables

   1 medium slice of broiled liver, or 6 ounces of broiled fish

   Lettuce salad, with low-calorie salad dressing if wanted

   1 serving of artificially sweetened gelatin dessert

   Beverage

Extra Snack

   ½ artificially sweetened or natural baked apple

Breakfast

   1 vitamin-mineral tablet

   1 egg poached, boiled, scrambled or fried in no-fat pan

   1 slice of extra-thin toast with artificially sweetened jam or jelly if desired

   1 glass skim milk

Lunch

   1 cup of bouillon, broth, or consommé

   8 medium-size shrimps with cocktail sauce on bed of lettuce

   2 pieces of melba toast

   Beverage

Dinner

- ½ cantaloupe with artificial sweetening if desired
- 6 ounces of broiled fish with fresh lemon juice, herbs, spices
- 1 cup chopped spinach (no butter or margarine)
- 1 serving of artificially sweetened gelatin dessert
- Beverage

Extra Snack

- 3 celery stalks stuffed with cottage cheese, sprinkled with paprika

SATURDAY

Breakfast

- 1 vitamin-mineral tablet
- 1 egg boiled, poached, scrambled or fried in no-fat pan
- 1 slice of extra-thin toast, with artificially sweetened jam or jelly if desired
- 1 glass skim milk

Lunch

- 1 cup of bouillon, broth, or consommé
- ½ can of water-packed tuna, or drained salmon, on bed of lettuce
- Beverage

Dinner

- 1 cup of bouillon, broth, or consommé
- 4 ounces of lean roast beef or steak, or 6 ounces of lobster meat
- Tossed salad, with low-calorie salad dressing if desired
- 1 serving of artificially sweetened gelatin dessert
- Beverage

Extra Snack

- ½ sliced orange or segments, when wanted

SUNDAY

Breakfast

- 1 vitamin-mineral tablet

1-egg fluffy omelet whipped with a little skim milk, in no-fat pan

1 slice of extra-thin toast, with artificially sweetened jam or jelly if desired

1 glass skim milk

Lunch

1 cup of bouillon, broth, or consommé

Tossed salad of greens and 2 slices of chicken or turkey cut up, with low-calorie salad dressing if wanted

2 pieces of melba toast

Beverage

Dinner

1 fresh fruit cup, natural or artificially sweetened

4 ounces of lean roast leg of lamb (no gravy), with artificially sweetened mint jelly or other jelly if desired

6 asparagus tips (no butter, margarine, or hollandaise sauce)

½ cup cooked, diced carrots

1 serving of artificially sweetened gelatin dessert

Beverage

Extra Snack

½ cantaloupe or wedge of other melon in season, when wanted

7-DAY QUICK VARIETY DIET . . . NO. 2

MONDAY

Breakfast

1 vitamin-mineral tablet

1 egg boiled, poached, scrambled or fried in no-fat pan

1 slice of extra-thin toast, with a little artificially sweetened jam or jelly if desired

1 glass skim milk

Lunch

1 cup clear clam broth or clam juice

10 to 12 medium-size shrimps with a little cocktail sauce

¼ small head of lettuce with low-calorie dressing, lemon juice, or vinegar with a touch of oil

Beverage

Dinner

1 cup of low-calorie bouillon, broth, or consommé

4 ounces of lean hamburger

1 cup of vegetable (or half-cups of 2 different vegetables); no avocados, no beans other than green or wax beans, no lentils, no potatoes, only small portions of peas

1 serving of artificially sweetened gelatin dessert

Beverage

Extra Snack

½ medium-size apple (have this extra snack mid-morning, mid-afternoon, or evening, as you please)

TUESDAY

Breakfast

1 vitamin-mineral tablet

4 tablespoons of cottage cheese, flavored with cinnamon and artificial sweetening if preferred

1 slice of extra-thin toast, with artificially sweetened jam or jelly if desired

1 glass skim milk

Lunch

1 cup of low-calorie bouillon, broth, or consommé

½ cantaloupe or other melon in season, with 2 tablespoons of cottage cheese in center

1 serving of artificially sweetened gelatin dessert

Beverage

Dinner

1 cup of bouillon, broth, or consommé

4 ounces of broiled lean steak or lean hamburger

Salad of ½ sliced tomato on lettuce leaves, with low-calorie salad dressing if desired

1 serving of artificially sweetened gelatin dessert
Beverage

Extra Snack

1 piece of fruit when wanted, your choice of a small-size apple, pear, orange, or banana

WEDNESDAY

Breakfast

1 vitamin-mineral tablet

1 egg scrambled in no-fat pan

1 slice of extra-thin toast with artificially sweetened jam or jelly if desired

1 glass skim milk

Lunch

1 cup of bouillon, broth, or consommé

1 hard-boiled egg, sliced, seasoned with herbs and spices if desired

3 stalks of celery spread lightly with cottage cheese, seasoned to taste

1 serving of artificially sweetened gelatin dessert
Beverage

Dinner

1 cup of bouillon, broth, or consommé

4 tablespoons of cottage cheese mixed with drained minced clams and seasoned to taste

6 medium-size lettuce leaves (under cottage cheese, as a salad)

2 pieces of melba toast

1 serving of artificially sweetened gelatin dessert
Beverage

Extra Snack

½ medium-size sliced orange, or tangerine segments, when desired

THURSDAY

Breakfast

1 vitamin-mineral tablet

2 tablespoons of cottage cheese, seasoned to taste

1 slice of extra-thin toast, with artificially sweetened jam or jelly if desired

1 glass skim milk

Lunch

1 cup of bouillon, broth, or consommé

Vegetable plate of 1 broiled tomato, ½ cup of spinach, ½ cup of green beans (or same portions of other low-calorie vegetables)

2 pieces of melba toast, with artificially sweetened jam or jelly if wanted

Beverage

Dinner

1 cup of bouillon, broth, or consommé

4 ounces of broiled lean hamburger

Wedge of lettuce with low-calorie salad dressing

1 serving of artificially sweetened gelatin dessert

Beverage

Extra Snack

4-ounce glass of buttermilk, or skim milk with artificially sweetened flavoring if desired

FRIDAY

Breakfast

1 vitamin-mineral tablet

1 egg poached, boiled, scrambled or fried in no-fat pan

1 slice of extra-thin toast, with artificially sweetened jam or jelly if desired

1 glass skim milk

Lunch

1 cup of bouillon, broth, or consommé

½ 8-oz. can of water-packed tuna, or drained salmon, seasoned to taste with fresh lemon juice, herbs, and spices

Lettuce salad with low-calorie salad dressing

Beverage

Dinner

1 cup of bouillon, broth, or consommé

118

Vegetable plate of half-cup servings of three low-calorie vegetables seasoned to taste (no butter or margarine)

1 serving of artificially sweetened gelatin dessert

Beverage

Extra Snack

2 soda biscuits spread with 1 tablespoon of cottage cheese, and artificially sweetened jam or jelly if desired

SATURDAY

Breakfast

1 vitamin-mineral tablet

½ grapefruit, with artificial sweetening if desired

2 pieces of melba toast moderately spread with cottage cheese or artificially sweetened jam or jelly

1 glass skim milk

Lunch

1 cup of bouillon, broth, or consommé

Salad of 1 sliced hard-boiled egg, ½ sliced tomato, on lettuce leaves, with low-calorie salad dressing if desired

½ baked apple, natural or with artificial sweetening

Beverage

Dinner

1 cup of bouillon, broth, or consommé

4 ounces of white-meat turkey or chicken, all skin removed

Small portion of artificially sweetened cranberry sauce or apple sauce

½ cup spinach

½ cup green beans

1 serving of artificially sweetened gelatin dessert

Beverage

Extra Snack

2 tablespoons of cottage cheese mixed with cinnamon or flavoring, artificially sweetened, to be eaten when desired

119

Breakfast

    1 vitamin-mineral tablet

    1 egg poached, boiled, scrambled or fried in no-fat pan

    1 slice of extra-thin toast, with artificially sweetened jam or jelly if desired

    1 glass skim milk

Lunch

    ½ 8-oz. can of water-packed tuna, or drained salmon, on lettuce leaves, with fresh lemon juice or low-calorie salad dressing

    1 carrot cut into strips

    Beverage

Dinner

    4 medium shrimps with a little cocktail sauce, on lettuce

    4 ounces of lean roast beef or steak (no gravy)

    2 half-cups of low-calorie vegetables (no butter or margarine)

    1 serving of artificially sweetened gelatin dessert

    Beverage

Extra Snack

    ½ sliced orange, when desired

7-DAY QUICK VARIETY DIET . . . NO. 3

Monday

Breakfast

    1 vitamin-mineral tablet

    1 egg boiled or poached, or scrambled or fried in a no-fat pan

    1 slice protein bread, with a little artificially sweetened jelly or jam, if desired

    1 glass skim milk

Lunch

    1 cup chicken consommé

    3 oz. lean hamburger

1 carrot cut in slim sticks
3 celery stalks
Beverage

Dinner
1 cup clear soup
4 oz. broiled swordfish steak
Tossed salad with lemon juice or low-calorie dressing
1 serving of artificially sweetened gelatin dessert
Beverage

TUESDAY

Breakfast
1 vitamin-mineral tablet
½ small orange
1 slice toast thinly spread with artificially sweetened
  jam or jelly
1 glass skim milk

Lunch
1 cup beef broth
Medium tomato stuffed with crabmeat
1 serving of artificially sweetened gelatin dessert
Beverage

Dinner
1 cup chicken consommé
¼ broiled chicken (6 oz.)
½ cup green beans
1 serving of artificially sweetened gelatin dessert
Beverage

WEDNESDAY

Breakfast
1 vitamin-mineral tablet
1 slice of toast thinly spread with artificially sweetened
  jam or jelly
1 glass skim milk

Lunch
1 cup clear soup
4-oz. broiled halibut

½ cup steamed carrots
1 serving of artificially sweetened gelatin dessert
Beverage

Dinner

1 cup beef bouillon
1 thin slice calf's liver (2 oz.), broiled
½ cup brussels sprouts
1 serving of artificially sweetened gelatin dessert
Beverage

THURSDAY

Breakfast

1 vitamin-mineral tablet
1 hard-boiled egg (or egg cooked as you wish, without
   fat added)
1 glass skim milk

Lunch

1 cup chicken consommé
3-inch wedge of melon or ½ orange, or cup of strawberries, no sugar
2 tablespoons creamed cottage cheese
1 slice of white, rye or whole wheat toast, plain
Beverage

Dinner

¾ cup all-vegetable soup
4 oz. lean hamburger, well broiled
6 spears asparagus
1 serving of artificially sweetened gelatin dessert
Beverage

FRIDAY

Breakfast

1 vitamin-mineral tablet
Half grapefruit
1 glass skim milk

Lunch

1 cup clear soup
4 oz. cold shrimp, with 1 tablespoon cocktail sauce

Lettuce leaves, moderate portion
1 slice of white, rye or whole wheat, plain or with
thinly spread artificially sweetened jelly or jam
1 serving artificially sweetened gelatin dessert
Beverage

Dinner
1 cup of clear broth
4 oz. veal, broiled
½ cup cauliflower
1 medium-size pickle, sour or dill
1 serving artificially sweetened gelatin dessert
Beverage

SATURDAY

Breakfast
1 vitamin-mineral tablet
½ cup orange juice
⅔ cup of oatmeal
1 8-oz. glass of skim milk (use some on oatmeal)
Beverage

Lunch
1 cup chicken consommé
1 hard-boiled egg, sliced thin
1 slice of white, rye or whole wheat, plain or with a
little artificially sweetened jelly or jam
1 serving artificially sweetened gelatin dessert
Beverage

Dinner
1 cup clam juice or clam broth
4 oz. flounder, broiled
Broiled tomato, medium-size
1 serving artificially sweetened gelatin dessert
Beverage

SUNDAY

Breakfast
1 vitamin-mineral tablet
1 egg, boiled or poached, or fried without fat

1 slice of white, rye or whole wheat, plain or with a little artificially sweetened jelly or jam

1 glass skim milk

Lunch

1 cup beef bouillon

Half cantaloupe or slice of other melon, or sliced half-orange, or half-cup berries

4 tablespoons creamed cottage cheese (in cantaloupe, if desired)

1 serving artificially sweetened gelatin dessert

Beverage

Dinner

1 cup clear soup

4 oz. lobster meat

1 medium tomato, sliced, with moderate portion of lettuce, with lemon juice or low-calorie dressing

2 slices melba toast, rye or white, plain or with a little artificially sweetened jelly or jam

Beverage

Where you are permitted a slice of bread, it may be toasted or not, as you wish.

To weigh ounces of food such as meat and fish, a small, inexpensive postal scale works out well.

If you want to skip any servings at any meal, that's fine; the less you eat, the quicker you'll lose weight.

Go to it now—and you'll see a slimmer you, *one week from today!*

THE QUICK VEGETABLE-FRUIT-PLUS-PROTEIN DIET

If you "love" vegetables, you could live by eating only the lower-calorie vegetables, just about as much as you could possibly consume. You would be slim all over, vigorous and healthy, for the rest of your life. You could eat as many of the lower-calorie vegetables as you want (avoiding the few higher-calorie vegetables such as avocados, beans, chickpeas, lentils, peas, sweet potatoes, and winter squash)—up to 6 meals a day—and still stay beautifully slim.

But—eating all vegetables of the lower-calorie types means exactly that—no butter, cheese, eggs, fats, margarine, nuts, oils, and so on. The true vegetarian consumes nothing but vegetables: those who add other foods such as eggs, milk products, and nuts are not true vegetarians. The only thing that need be added to the vegetables is *plenty* of liquid—lots of water daily, plus "no-calorie" sodas, and coffee and tea without milk, cream, or sugar (the coffee and tea are by choice, and are not necessary).

Natural fruits, without sugar added (artificial sweetening is okay), also are low in calories and can be part of a vegetable-and-fruit diet, or an all-fruit diet. However, with fruits, you cannot eat "all you want," but should count calories in order not to exceed your daily reducing total (600–900 calories) or the maintenance total that will keep you at your ideal weight according to your height, as figured by the ideal weight chart in Chapter 2.

I don't recommend an all-vegetable or all-fruit diet for teenagers. During your growing years, you require more protein than is provided by eating only vegetables and fruits. For you who like vegetables and fruits so much that you could practically live on them alone so far as eating preference goes, I have devised here a Quick Vegetable-Fruit-Plus-Protein Diet. It meets all my requirements for the essentials that will reduce you healthfully and surely. Since the daily total is only about 600–700 calories, this diet will reduce you quickly. You will lose enough pounds per week to keep you reducing until you are down to ideal weight and attractive slimness.

Vary this diet with the Quick Teenage Diet for excellent results, if you prefer, as many of my teenage dieters have done. Go on the Quick Teenage Diet for a week, concentrating on meats, fish, eggs, cottage cheese, and other proteins that take off fat in a hurry. Then, if you have a craving for vegetables and fruits, switch for a week to the Vegetable-Fruit-Plus-Protein Diet.

The next week (if you are still overweight), go back to the meats, chicken, and other proteins on the Quick Teenage Diet. This turnabout results in speedy weight loss if it suits your individual preference. And I never forget that the whole purpose of this book in your case is *to slim you personally*, rather than to apply any hard-and-fast formula for all teenagers.

Drink at least 8 glasses of liquids per day—including water (the best of all), "no-calorie" artificially sweetened sodas of all flavors (and club soda, of course), and coffee and tea without milk, cream, or sugar, if you are normally a coffee and tea drinker. (You may add a dash of skim milk or non-dairy creamer to coffee and tea, if you wish.) In addition, you should drink an 8-ounce glass of skim milk per day as specified in the listing—and add a second glass of skim milk daily if you are under age 18. Have your skim milk at any time of day or evening you prefer, at meals or between meals.

Take a vitamin-mineral tablet daily, as specified in the listing. I have never found a single teenager on this diet to be vitamin-deficient, but I prefer that you take the extra vitamins and minerals nevertheless. Don't take more vitamins and minerals than the usual daily tablet, capsule, or liquid—whatever form you prefer—since problems may arise from overdosing your system with excess synthetic vitamins and minerals on any daily eating regime.

You may switch to other vegetables, fruits, and protein foods than those in the 7-Day listing, but don't exceed the calorie count as you substitute a different serving. For instance, instead of a cup of broccoli you could substitute a cup of spinach, since both have about the same calorie count (see calorie chart to aid in your selection). Instead of the 3-ounce lean hamburger, you could substitute 3 ounces of broiled chicken or turkey, totaling about the same in calories. You could replace a medium-size baked apple with a medium-size sliced orange, about the same calorie total. Refer to your calorie tables, but always substitute the same type of food—a protein serving for another protein portion, vegetable for vegetable, fruit for fruit. This assures sufficient protein intake for the needs of your growing body—*not* growing in excess fat on this diet, but slimming down beautifully.

You may use seasonings, herbs, spices (but never salt foods too heavily), and a little (never a lot) of mustard, ketchup, chili sauce, cocktail sauce. You are permitted a little vinegar, or low-calorie salad dressing (truly low calorie; check product labels), always in moderation lest you load on too many calories and slow up the quick-reducing process.

You may snack on small portions of raw vegetables such as carrots, radishes, cauliflower, cucumber, celery. You may also have a cup of no-fat consommé, broth, bouillon, or any clear no-fat soup, when you wish.

Here is your daily listing—and remember, you are not permitted any butter, margarine, oils, or any fats, no heavy gravies or dressings on vegetables or any other foods. You may switch Monday for Tuesday, repeat any one day instead of another, as you desire, according to what foods are available where and when you eat, at home, at school, or eating out anywhere (this is true of any of my 7-Day or other diets).

MONDAY

Breakfast
1 vitamin-mineral tablet
2 oz. orange juice (no sugar added)
1 egg, prepared any way without any fats at all
1 glass skim milk

Lunch
1 cup chicken consommé (fat removed)

Vegetable plate of 1 cup broccoli, 1 cup green beans,
1 medium-size broiled tomato, and 1 sliced hard-
boiled egg

1 serving artificially sweetened gelatin dessert

Beverage

Dinner

1 cup beef broth

3 oz. broiled lean hamburger

Salad of medium sliced tomato, ¼ medium compact
head of lettuce, 6 raw radishes

1 serving artificially sweetened gelatin dessert

Beverage

TUESDAY

Breakfast

1 vitamin-mineral tablet

Half grapefruit (no sugar; artificial sweetening okay)

1 egg (prepared any way you wish without fat)

1 glass skim milk

Lunch

1 cup beef bouillon

Salad plate of ½ medium-size compact head of lettuce,
a sliced medium-size tomato, a medium-size raw
carrot cut in strips or round slices, 2 stalks of celery

3 oz. creamed cottage cheese (on salad plate, if preferred)

1 serving artificially sweetened gelatin dessert

Beverage

Dinner

1 cup chicken consommé

4 oz. broiled fish with drops of fresh lemon juice

1 cup spinach, 6 medium asparagus spears

Baked apple, medium size (no sugar added, artificial
sweetening okay)

Beverage

Breakfast
  1 vitamin-mineral tablet
  Half cantaloupe (or other melon)
  1 egg
  1 glass skim milk

Lunch
  1 cup beef bouillon
  Salad plate of bed of lettuce, 1 medium-size sliced
     tomato, sliced carrot, sliced cucumber, and 1 sliced
     hard-boiled egg
  1 serving artificially sweetened gelatin dessert
  Beverage

Dinner
  1 cup chicken broth
  3 oz. steak
  1 medium-size broiled tomato, 1 cup brussels sprouts
  1 serving artificially sweetened gelatin dessert
  Beverage

Breakfast
  1 vitamin-mineral tablet
  1 medium-size orange, sliced
  1 glass skim milk

Lunch
  1 cup chicken consommé
  1 poached egg, with 1 cup cauliflower, ½ cup boiled
     onions, 1 cup wax beans
  1 serving artificially sweetened gelatin dessert
  Beverage

Dinner
  1 cup beef broth
  4 oz. sliced chicken (or chicken leg)
  6 medium asparagus tips
  1 cup summer squash
  1 serving artificially sweetened gelatin dessert

FRIDAY

Breakfast
1 vitamin-mineral tablet
4 oz. orange juice
1 egg
1 glass skim milk

Lunch
1 cup beef bouillon
1 mixed salad of lettuce, cubes of 1 medium-size tomato, 1 carrot sliced, 2 stalks cubed celery, 2 sliced radishes
3 oz. creamed cottage cheese
1 serving artificially sweetened gelatin dessert
Beverage

Dinner
1 cup clam chowder (no fat or potatoes) or clam broth
4 oz. broiled fish
1 cup spinach, 1 cup green beans
1 cup cubed pineapple (no sugar)
Beverage

SATURDAY

Breakfast
1 vitamin-mineral tablet
1 medium-size orange, sliced (or peach)
1 egg
1 glass skim milk

Lunch
1 cup chicken broth
1 salad plate of bed of lettuce, 6 medium-size asparagus spears, 1 medium-size quartered tomato, 1 carrot, 1 cucumber, 1 medium-size sweet pepper, sliced
1 serving artificially sweetened gelatin dessert
Beverage

Dinner
1 cup beef bouillon
3 oz. roast beef (or other lean sliced meat)
1 small boiled potato, 1 cup broccoli, 4 oz. sauerkraut

1 serving artificially sweetened gelatin dessert
Beverage

SUNDAY

Breakfast
1 vitamin-mineral tablet
Half grapefruit (no sugar)
1 glass skim milk

Lunch
1 cup beef broth
1 poached egg on 1 cup spinach, with 1 cup diced cooked carrots, 1 cup boiled cabbage
1 serving artificially sweetened gelatin dessert
Beverage

Dinner
1 cup chicken consommé
1 cup summer squash, 1 cup green beans
1 medium-size sliced tomato on lettuce leaves
1 serving artificially sweetened gelatin dessert
Beverage

LIQUIDS-ONLY 1-DAY SUPER-QUICK DIET

This is an excellent 1-day diet that will take off 2 or more pounds in a day (depending on how overweight you are). You can work in this 1-Day Liquids-Only Diet during any week on any kind of dieting, whatever day you choose, if you want to speed up your weight loss. Since you don't eat any solid foods, your system gets a healthful rest and change, and any feeling at all of bloat and discomfort due to excess weight is likely to vanish rapidly.

Use this diet for 1 day only, then go back on the Quick Teenage Diet, or whichever of my rapid reducing diets you are using.

Follow these simple instructions:

1. Don't eat any solid food at all during the day of relief.
2. Keep drinking large quantities of liquids hour after hour, an 8-ounce glass at least every 2 waking hours, preferably at least in each hour.
3. Drink at least 8 to 10 glasses of water daily, more if you can.
4. Drink 3 cups each day of low-calorie bouillon, broth, or consommé, made with half again as much water as noted in package directions. This provides more liquid per portion, and milder flavor.
5. Drink your fill of artificially sweetened carbonated beverages in all flavors, also club soda (no beverages containing sugar, milk, or cream).
6. Drink plenty of coffee (no-caffeine coffee, if you prefer) and tea, cup after cup, artificially sweetened if you like, but no sugar, milk, or cream (if you drink coffee and tea normally).
7. Have a glass of skim milk during the day (2 glasses if you are under age 18).
8. Have a vitamin-mineral tablet first thing in the morning.
9. Get your average amount of daily activity—walking, working, but avoid strenuous exercising.
10. To repeat, don't stay on the Liquids-Only Diet more than one day during each week. If you drink enough fluids, as advised, you won't crave solid food, since you'll have a feeling of being full.

Slimmed Down Beautifully, After
6 Years of Failure

You can be confident that any of my rapid-reducing methods will work for you, as they have for others. Letters reporting success come in daily, thrilling always to me, and containing special inspiration for you. Here's a typical comment from a young woman:

"I'm so grateful that I must take two minutes to thank you for your speedy weight loss diet methods. I'd been *trying,* without accomplishing it, to lose weight *for 6 years up to now* (since age 13). Your diet has certainly proved successful for me. Since I took off the extra pounds, I'm able to work for TWA Airlines. I can't thank you enough for your methods for losing weight."

The same wonderful success can be yours, so don't delay another day in starting your selected speedy weight-loss program. Thousands upon thousands of teenagers have succeeded in trimming down beautifully, so "go thou and do likewise." Slim and trim on whichever of the diets in this book appeals to you most, personally. My prime recommendation again is the Quick Teenage Diet, which you can use week after week, or alternate with one or more of the other diets here.

However, the all-important criterion is what works best for you as an individual. Choose from these diets according to your own free will, knowing for sure that where there's a will, there's eventual ideal weight and slimness for you.

9

Anti-Acne Clear Skin Diet...
and Other Tips

It's not true that "beauty's but skin deep," for—as another proverb points out—"a fair skin may cover a pitted mind." It's also far from a certainty that being slim and having a clear complexion can solve all of life's problems and assure happiness, but they help. The Quick Teenage Diet will slim you down if you cooperate fully ... and my Anti-Acne Clear Skin Diet, *along with the right treatment by a dermatologist,* can clear up acne in a great majority of cases.

The worst thing you can do about an acne condition is to ignore it, or to figure that "it will clear up as I grow out of my teens." You can't count on acne to disappear as you get older if the basic conditions causing it are not corrected. You *can* be very optimistic about getting rid of acne starting right now, if you do something about it. As two leading dermatologists have stated positively in a book on skin problems: "You have a far better than even chance of the acne condition clearing up—*it does in over 75 percent of all cases with proper treatment and care.*"

Two Steps to Take Right Now
to Help Clear Up Acne

1. See a dermatologist—without question. The dermatologist is the medical specialist in the care and treatment of the skin (*derma*). He can advise and help you on every aspect of the treatment of acne and other skin problems, in addition to diet, which is one phase. In addition to advising how to clear up your skin, he can help prevent scars from forming from a severe acne condition. The experienced dermatologist frequently can also use modern techniques to correct and improve any past scarring from acne.

2. *Slim down quickly* by following my Anti-Acne Clear Skin Diet advice, beginning now. While taking off excess weight is no guarantee that acne and related skin problems will be corrected, removing extra fat and flab is indicated for skin health and total good health. As your unwanted fat vanishes all over your body, the tissue fat also is decreased under the skin of the face and elsewhere. Effective reducing tends to diminish the amount of fat and perspiration, along with secretions from the oil glands of the skin.

Through the years I have found with teenage patients afflicted with acne that *getting down to ideal weight is an important and usually essential part of the treatment for clearing up an acne condition and promoting a clear, healthy complexion.* Don't bypass this step—start on your anti-acne reducing program now. There's a good chance that you'll see improvement in a very short time.

There have been some medical people more recently who state that acne is not affected by diet, but my actual patient experience is otherwise. Like many dermatologists and other doctors, I have found that more overweight teenagers have acne and other skin eruptions than those of ideal weight. Also, many know—based on successes in clearing up acne—that low-fat, low-sugar eating is generally a big help in improving the complexion and eliminating many skin problems.

This letter from a young man tells of what frequently happens in checking skin troubles: "I'm a 16-year-old who has had acne for 4 years. I've tried various treatments and medications. Nothing had proved effective. I had gotten to the point where I was very discouraged and self-conscious. Three weeks ago I went on your anti-acne diet. Right now my skin is in as good condition as I can remember. I have also lost many pounds and inches around the waist . . . The way things are going, my skin should be almost pimple-free within a few weeks."

While I cannot promise that my anti-acne diet will be a "guaranteed cure-all," it will certainly slim you speedily and should help clear up your skin, along with other treatment by a dermatologist.

ANTI-ACNE CLEAR SKIN DIET

The best diet in my experience to help clear up acne and other skin blemishes, as it slims you, is my basic Quick Teenage Diet—*along with a few essential changes.* Reread carefully the basic Quick Teenage Diet in Chapter 4, and eat accordingly, but note these vital differences for your Anti-Acne Clear Skin Diet.

1. Don't eat any shellfish—no seafood such as clams, crab, lobster, oysters, shrimp. The iodides in these foods seem to aggravate the acne. You may enjoy fresh fish broiled, boiled, or baked, without butter, margarine, or any fats (never fried in fats).

2. Don't use iodized salt. Be sure to check the salt that is used for you at home, both at the table and in cooking (ask at the store, if you're not sure). If you find that it's iodized, switch to plain, *non-iodized* salt (you won't detect any difference in flavor). In any case, avoid the use of much salt, as well as salty foods.

3. Don't use any spicy sauces such as ketchup, mustard, chili sauce, and relishes.

4. In drinking skim milk, it's preferable to boil the milk first (1 glass a day if 18 years old or over, 2 glasses a day if under age 18). You can boil the day's quantity of skim milk ahead of time and chill it in the refrigerator for use when you want it (warm or hot boiled skim milk is okay, also).

5. In drinking sodas, choose only the "no-calorie" artificially sweetened beverages—*but not cola or chocolate flavoring*, not even in the no-sugar sodas. Don't drink any sodas or other beverages containing sugar, certainly never cola, chocolate, coffee-flavored, or cocoa.

6. *Don't drink coffee at all.* You may have tea (if you drink tea normally) but be sure it is weak tea, never strong.

7. *"NO" foods that are not permitted* in anti-acne eating, in addition to those already mentioned, include:

✳ NO fats, not even the fats in whole milk and whole milk cheeses, cream, butter, margarine, oils, bacon fat, chicken fat, any fats

✳ NO mayonnaise, rich dressings, gravies

✳ NO chocolate or other candy; no cocoa

✳ NO cakes, cookies, pastries, pies, icing

✳ NO fried foods, no pizzas or other crusty foods

✳ NO nuts, no peanuts or peanut butter

✳ No highly seasoned or spiced foods, no smoked meats, fish, or other smoked, spicy foods

✳ NO fatty meats such as bacon, ham, pork

✳ NO sodas or other beverages containing sugar

✳ NO cola drinks at all, no coffee

✳ NO alcoholic beverages, not even light wines or beer

Important Anti-Acne Dieting Checkpoints

Checking the basic Quick Teenage Diet listing, along with the restrictions for acne, blemishes, and other such skin problems, you may enjoy the following on your Anti-Acne Clear Skin Diet:

▪ SKIM MILK, 1 or 2 glasses a day, depending on your age, pre-boiling the skim milk

▪ LEAN MEATS . . . beef, lamb, veal (no fats used in preparation)

▪ CHICKEN, TURKEY (all skin removed, no fats used in preparation)

■ LEAN FISH, but *no* shellfish (no fats used in preparation)

■ EGGS (any style prepared without fats)

■ COTTAGE CHEESE, also pot cheese and farmer cheese (but no other cheeses)

■ VITAMIN-MINERAL TABLET DAILY, plus a vitamin A tablet every day

■ "NO-CALORIE" SODAS (but no cola, chocolate, or coffee flavors; all other flavors okay, and club soda)

■ WATER, at least eight 8-ounce glasses per day. Drinking lots of water daily is excellent for the complexion in general. One "beauty expert" states, in advising water enthusiastically for "skin beauty": "I call this the non-vitamin vitamin. Cold, crystal-clear water is a positive beauty tonic for your skin. Drink 8 glasses of water every day. That's an absolute minimum. Water flushes the poisonous substances out of our systems." I wouldn't put it quite that way, but water is certainly a "must" for speedy reducing, and a positive aid for skin health and a good complexion.

■ ARTIFICIALLY SWEETENED GELATIN DESSERT, up to 2 servings a day, at meals or between meals. But don't add any sauces or toppings, and don't use chocolate or coffee flavored gelatin dessert, or any over 12 calories per serving.

■ BOUILLON, BROTH, CONSOMMÉ, up to 3 cups per day—homemade without any fats, or made with fat-free cubes, liquids, or powders.

Make up your own daily meals from these permitted foods for your eating on the Anti-Acne Clear Skin Diet. You may choose the Super-Quick Teenage Diet (Chapter 5), or you may use the 7-Day Quick Teenage Diets (Chapter 6). Simply make the slight revisions by avoiding those few foods and flavorings not permitted on the Anti-Acne Clear Skin Diet, as detailed in this chapter.

If You Want Vegetables and Fruits

There is no reason for most teenagers with acne to go without fruits and vegetables, so long as the daily calorie intake is kept under 700 calories (have a doctor check you after four weeks, although you should be feeling very well and losing pounds and inches rapidly). If you feel that you "must" have vegetables and fruits every day, I recommend that you use one of these diets to slim quickly and also help combat and clear up acne and other skin troubles:

1. *Go on the QUICK TEENAGE DIVIDEND DIET,* following the detailed instructions in Chapter 7. Make your daily dividend a vegetable or fruit of your choice. Keep on the diet faithfully and you'll have your fruits and vegetables, you'll help clear up your skin problems, and you'll lose those excess pounds and inches in a hurry.

2. *Or, use the QUICK VEGETABLE-FRUIT-PLUS PROTEIN DIET* in Chapter 8. This is also a helpful anti-acne diet, and will change your unwanted personal *inflation* into the wonderful *deflation* you want for your figure as you slim down. You'll see heartening results—day after day—as pounds and inches vanish.

Other Anti-Acne Guidelines

* *Keep active, but don't exercise violently.* Brisk walking every day, swimming, bicycling, general calisthenics, are all beneficial for losing weight and for your general health. Try to avoid violent exercise and activity that may cause excessive perspiration and probable increased activity of the oil glands. Wash and dry skin thoroughly after exercising.

* *Wash your face and adjacent areas* at least 3 times daily with mild antiseptic soap—but just lather up and smooth with your hands on your face, don't scrub hard, don't use a brush on your skin. Shampoo your hair 2 to

3 times a week to help remove excess oiliness from hair and scalp.

✳ *Don't use heavy creams or excessive make-up.* If any, use fat-free lotions and creams on your face, and make up as lightly as possible.

✳ *Wash your hands as often as necessary* in order to keep them clean. Try not to touch your face and other areas with eruptions; thus you help avoid development of acne pustules.

✳ *In respect to "anti-acne preparations"* offered in stores, some of these may be helpful, but I urge you to see a dermatologist or your doctor and get his advice about what preparations to use. He may prescribe more effective medications that you can't get without a prescription. Many advances have been made, including use of antibiotics, vitamin A, vitamin C, and other medications, and various improved forms of treatment. Why put up with half-measures when the dermatologist is trained to help you to the fullest possible degree? He will advise you not only on acne, but also on any skin problems that you may have, think you have, or are afraid of getting.

✳ *Comb your hair to keep it off your face* as much as possible. Heavy, low bangs on the forehead, long hair styles for males as well as females, tend to increase chances of acne and other skin problems. In combing and styling your hair, try to avoid contact of oily hair with skin. Don't use heavy, oily hair dressings. Combat dandruff and oily particles on the scalp.

✳ *Don't remove blackheads yourself,* as doing this improperly can bring out worse eruptions. Your doctor will remove the blackheads and perhaps show you how to do it correctly yourself, so that you avoid inflaming problem spots further. Don't rub or pick on inflamed spots or areas.

✳ *Don't worry or be nervous* about common fallacies in connection with acne. Learn the truth in your visit to the doctor (nervous tension speeds up activity of oil

141

and sweat glands, and may bring on more skin problems). For instance, acne is not caused by more or less sexual activity. Acne is not "catching," so don't be at all concerned about that.

* *Don't be discouraged* if with proper diet, treatment, and care, your skin problems seem to improve and then flare up occasionally. Double-check what you're doing, stay precisely on your diet (if you've indulged in forbidden foods, just shrug it off, and concentrate on eating correctly from now on). An occasional setback is to be expected, but you should improve steadily by sticking to the correct eating and treatment routines until your skin is cleared up beautifully.

* *After you are slim and trim,* if acne hasn't been cleared up entirely, keep in mind that this same selection of foods can be continued to help correct and guard against skin problems. On Keep-Slim Eating, avoid the fatty, sugary foods, as advised on the preceding pages.

TRIPLE Rewards from Anti-Acne Dieting

You'll get special satisfaction from the results of anti-acne dieting in these three inspiring ways:

1. You'll see improvement in your skin condition soon after you switch to my low-fat, low-sugar eating recommendations, along with treatment and care advised following a visit to a dermatologist.

2. Right from the first day that you go on one of my anti-acne diets, you'll see your weight dropping on the scale. That provides a glow of satisfaction that you are moving toward your goal of a slim figure as well as a clear skin. The rapid weight loss is your "built-in will power" to keep going and to keep accomplishing through your own fine efforts and volition.

3. There's a tremendous lift in your spirits and self-respect when you're on an effective course of action. You personally have selected, from the choices in this

book, the plan of action that will work best for you. And you know that the doubly wonderful part of your dieting is that you're going to help clear up your skin problems and lift off your overweight burden—for *doubly* beautiful results.

10

Slimming, Trimming Benefits of Activity and Exercise

If you're overweight and underexercised, you're never going to be able to touch your toes by letting your fingernails grow longer. Not that it's so important to be able to touch your toes without bending your knees, but keeping your body active and well exercised is a vital aid in attaining the slim, trim figure you want. (Of course, if you have any heart, lung, or other impairment, you will not be exercising or dieting except with the advice of your personal physician.)

I certainly don't urge that you become a super athlete or gymnast, not at all. I'm against *over*exercise, which can cause bulging muscles, adding excess pounds and inches. I do want you to learn the simple, easy ways to use your body well physically, enough to help use up extra calories for most efficient and effective reducing.

Make no mistake about this: You cannot get rid of a lot of overweight simply through exercise and activity—that must be combined with my rapid-reducing methods. The Quick Teenage Diet (or others of my speedy diets in this book) will take off the excess pounds of fat, while using your body actively will help trim off the flab faster and firm your slimmer figure. You'll find out here how to use your body actively and healthfully for extra figure-trimming results, without hours of boring calisthenics.

Getting your body into action properly and effectively can be simple and enjoyable, and will reward you through all the years ahead. Most important is doing the kind of exercise every day that you enjoy most, and doing it at least 15 minutes at a time continuously. You don't have to do push-ups. Choose the activity that pleases you most, personally, from those recommended in this chapter.

There are added benefits from keeping active. Dr. Charles Edwards, head of the U.S. Food and Drug Administration, stated, "Exercise is probably the greatest tension reliever I know of." Another noted health authority said, "Exercise is a definite help in reducing—one reason is that you can't very well eat while you are exercising."

The right activity and exercise also help you develop freedom and grace of movement as you slim down. *Get moving* as you start dieting. Tackle the whole slimming-activity program not as a chore, but as a way to the goal you want so much. It's not so tough; your attitude can make all the difference.

What Physical Activity Does for You

Activity, exercise, sports, and games involving running around perform many healthful functions in addition to improving your circulation. Physical activity burns up a great deal of the stored fat in your body as it tones your muscles. It softens the fat in the tissues, converting it easily to fatty acids. As you keep moving, and continue exercising regularly, flab disappears and your normal slim contours appear—the way you want them to be, firm and attractive.

Your new-found activity and exercise make it doubly vital that you drink lots of water as recommended on all the speedy weight-loss diets. When fat is burned for energy, and perspiration is increased, fatty acids flood the circulation and should be washed out continuously. I don't urge extremely strenuous exercise in hot weather, bringing on excessive perspiration (then some salt and potassium are necessary for the system). But keep moving, keep the water flowing, and fatty acids and fat will keep flowing from your body for rapid slimming and increased energy.

The third factor I urge in utilizing and burning up calories most effectively is deep-breathing (QTD Oxygen Exercise in Chapter 1). This also benefits you further by counteracting the oxygen deficit in the muscle tissue as you move around and exercise. All three—QTD eating, activity, proper breathing—combine for the most desirable, most effective, reducing program, all yours for wonderful benefits starting now.

Most Teenagers Are NOT Well Exercised

If you tend to sit around or lie around instead of moving around, you're no different from many other teenagers. You can blame TV, radio, records, automobiles, other modern-day features, for the decreased activity of many teenagers today. Lying around and watching TV, listening to radio and records or tapes, are enjoyable pastimes—nothing wrong with them, except when they tend to bring on that dread fattening and weakening disease *"Homo Sedentarious"* ("man sitting," instead of "man alive!"). It's not a question of eliminating TV and music, but of *adding* exercise daily.

The automobile promotes inactivity by carrying you even on a short move of only a couple of blocks, preventing your muscles from getting a needed workout. The elevator lifts you up and lets you down (in many ways) by keeping you from climbing the stairs. Combined with lounging around, the result too often is that muscles are weak and flabby, and few calories are used up.

You don't have to undertake a strenuous exercise or training program as professional athletes do. Just get up on your toes in every way, straighten and lift your posture, change your sedentary habits. Walk when you can, instead of riding. Climb a few flights of stairs, instead of using the elevator. Do the simple exercises suggested later in the chapter as you watch TV or listen to radio and records. Dance energetically (an increasing pleasure as your figure slims and becomes light and graceful). Think *action*.

It's sad as well as funny when somebody says about an overweight teenager, "The only exercise he gets is watching TV horror shows and letting his flesh creep." Another teen complained, "I wish I walked in my sleep so that I could get my exercise and rest at the same time." Once you experience the joy of having a slim, active body, you'll never sit around again.

Don't believe the old complaint that "exercise increases my appetite and makes me eat more." That isn't true. It's just another excuse for stuffing in food. Exercise may produce some muscle fatigue, which is normal but should not accelerate the appetite. Instead of food, fill up with water and no-calorie beverages.

Nor can you count on exercise to use up the calories packed in with an after-sports snack; you'd have to run steadily for almost 10 minutes to use up the calories in just one frankfurter without a roll. (On the other hand, it would take two whole hours of lying around to use up the calories of that one naked frankfurter!) Exercise is a very valuable aid, but never a substitute for QTD dieting.

Start with Improved Posture

Try to get in the habit of standing properly so that you *look* slimmer even before you start ("instant slimming," you might call this). Stand with your feet 6 to 12 inches apart, toes pointed straight ahead. Pull your abdomen (belly) in. Tuck your buttocks in toward the front. Lift your shoulders back. Raise your chest as though you're trying to touch your chin with it, as your chin lifts to a right angle with your neck. Try to promote that posture sitting, standing, walking—1, 2, 3—(1) abdomen in, (2) shoulders up and back, (3) chest lifted as though trying to touch your chin.

You'll look better instantly with this 1-2-3 improved posture, and you'll look slimmer and more alert and attractive instantly. What's more, you'll *feel* better as good posture becomes a habit with you. By the end of just one week on the Quick Teenage Diet, carrying yourself with uplifted posture, you'll be thrilled at the marvelous transformation in your figure.

QTD Oxygen Exercise . . . Isometrically

" 'Tis the breathing time of day with me," Shakespeare wrote. As I've advised before, your exercise "breathing time" is at least five to six times a day to expand your lungs and burn up calories more effectively. I recommend that you combine some *isometrics* with your regular QTD Oxygen Exercise to get additional good from it.

There are two basic types of exercise: (1) *Isometric* exercise concentrates on muscle contraction with little motion, and is generally to be done very briefly. (2) *Isotonic* exercise (a more effective aid in slimming, trimming, and promoting circulation) involves continuous action over a prolonged period, preferably at least 15 minutes at a time, as in walking, participating in active sports, and calisthenics involving lots of motion. Both isometric and isotonic actions play a vital role in promoting good health.

Here are the simple instructions for the QTD Oxygen Exercise—isometrically:

1. Stand in the erect posture position described earlier in this chapter.

2. Stiffen your arms at your sides, clench your fists as hard as possible.

3. To a slow count of 5, breathe in deeply with your mouth open, while you push back with your arms held stiff, fists clenched, as far back as possible while keeping

149

posture erect. Hold that position for an additional slow count to 3.

4. Expel your breath, loosen your fists and arms, returning arms to sides in natural hanging position.

5. Repeat this count-to-5 routine 5 times, pausing a few seconds after each exercise.

6. Repeat this 5-time isometric breathing exercise 5 to 6 times a day.

The regular QTD Oxygen Exercise can be done more readily, since you may do it sitting or lying down, as well as standing. I prefer that you substitute this isometric variation whenever possible. Once you make this daily breathing exercise a natural part of your everyday life, you'll soon find your breathing improving. You should also feel greater energy and vitality, and—take my word for it, based on my findings with overweight teenagers— it's a positive aid in speeding your reducing process.

Walking . . . Your Best Exercise

You don't need any special equipment for walking; it's all "built in," so that you're almost born walking—and you're meant to keep it up for the rest of your life, as too few do. You may be amused in this modern day by Thomas Jefferson's comments on walking:

"Walking is the best possible exercise. Habituate yourself to walk very far. The Europeans value themselves as having subdued the horse to the uses of man; but I doubt whether we have not lost more than we have gained by the uses of this animal." I wonder what Jefferson would think of the use of the mechanical "animals" we have now—the auto, plane, bus, train, motorcycle—and how these contraptions have cut down on human locomotion.

I agree with the great President, and particularly everyone who knows anything about good health, that "walking is the best possible exercise." So important to you in getting down to your desired weight and figure, purposeful walking for the sake of reducing helps trim off excess pounds and inches in a number of ways. Like other effective exercise, walking speeds up your metabolism, increasing the rate at which your body burns up food and pulls fat from the storage pockets.

This accelerated metabolism lasts not only while you're walking (or enjoying other good exercise) but for hours afterward, and just about continuously if you exercise enough. But to get the most out of walking, you must do more than just stick out one foot and then the other. Here's how simple it is to walk and get the wanted slimming effects best:

1. *Walk in the proper posture position*—abdomen in . . . shoulders back and up . . . chest lifted as though trying to touch your chin . . . head erect (not an exaggerated effect; this will become your natural, graceful, easy posture). That lifting of your chest will make you feel that you're sort of lifted from the ground as you walk.

2. *Walk briskly*—since sauntering does you little good in the way of exercising. Do NOT pump your arms and legs in an accented way, but stride along purposefully, enjoying moving your arms and legs energetically. Add a little "bounce" to your stride. You can almost feel the blood flow speeding up and coursing through your body, boosting your metabolism and burning up the fat in your body.

3. *Walk 15 minutes or more at a time*, whenever possible. The continuous motion and the moving of your arms and legs, speed and expand the circulation. It also sends healthful fresh supplies of blood through your body, helping to clear out fats and waste matter.

4. *Repeat your walking periods* as often as possible, to tone up your system and use up the most calories. Whenever you can, when you're invited or tempted to ride, walk instead—it's great for your figure. And, unlike strenuous exercises, walking firms the muscles of your legs without causing them to bulge or increase in size— quite the opposite. Walk with a companion for company

when convenient. But, above all, don't lag or sag along—*walk as though you mean it*!

5. *Walking exercise indoors* is also desirable, preferably in a large room. Stand in the right-hand front corner of the room. Walk *backwards* as far as possible . . . then sideways to your left as far as you can . . . then *forward* as far front as possible . . . then *sideways* to your right, to your original starting point. Keep this up for 15 minutes or more, moving energetically with vigor and bounce. Walking *backwards* helps reduce the buttocks particularly . . . walking *sideways* is an excellent plus in trimming your thighs and buttocks. If you place a TV set at the front of the room and watch a program (your eyes are fixed on the screen as your body moves around the room), the time will pass quickly.

Jogging is an effective form of exercise, but I don't recommend it unless you follow a proper, detailed jogging program that starts slowly with walking and a little jogging, then gradually increases until you're jogging fully only by the end of about a *year*. There have been some deaths reported from heart failure of men who started jogging fully at once, without the many months of gradual acceleration required for safety. For overweight teenagers I favor brisk walking, rather than unsupervised jogging or sustained running.

There's much pleasure in walking for physical and mental enjoyment, knowing as you stride that you're helping yourself lose weight. There are many added pleasures to discover constantly, walking in city or country. A perceptive young lady wrote, "Today I have grown taller from walking with the trees."

Swimming for Slimness

Swimming is a great exercise and sport for you to consider, whether in the ocean, a lake, or an indoor or outdoor pool. You can go far beyond just swimming, and take advantage of the opportunity to trim your figure through extra exercise in the water, daily if possible.

However, don't think you're getting much benefit if you simply loll around the pool, or plunge in and then hop out after a lap or two. Nor do you do much for your figure if you race a splashing length or two of the pool and then quit and lie puffing alongside the water. Sprawling for hours on a beach doesn't help, either. You probably are having fun, and that's all to the good, but you're not doing much to get rid of excess ounces, let alone inches.

For the most effective slimming activity in water, combine the following exercise with swimming; actually you can do the refreshing, calorie-consuming exercise even if you can't swim.

❋ *Swinging-Bobbing Exercise:* Stand in the water to a depth a few inches higher than your navel. Stiffen your arms at your sides and raise them slowly sideways until your outstretched hands meet above your head.

Now, as you slowly lower your stiffened arms outwards to your sides, bend your knees slowly at the same time, not into a full knee bend but until you're in a half-squatting position—with the water reaching about up to your shoulders—and your arms now all the way down at your sides.

Next, push yourself slowly upwards again, legs straightening, arms raising sideways, until you're standing erect once more, hands touching above your head.

Hold that position for about 3 seconds, then repeat the arm-lowering, knee-bending . . . then up and back to standing again. Continue that up-and-down, slow bobbing routine—10 times.

Now swim steadily with a relaxed, continuous stroke for a few minutes (if you're a swimmer). Then stop and go through the swinging-bobbing exercise 10 times again.

Keep up the swimming-then-exercising schedule for a total of 15 minutes, taking it easy, not letting yourself get exhausted. At the end of the quarter-hour, you'll be well exercised.

Continue swimming, resting and enjoying yourself as long as you wish, knowing that you've had a very helpful 15-minute slimming, trimming workout. This will help firm your body and take off excess inches faster while you are following your Quick Teenage Diet program.

Bicycling, Skiing, Rowing . . . and More

Choose the exercise-activity that suits you best from the many available. The main thing is to make a start, to get out there and *do it*, and then keep doing it another day—and another—and another. As in dieting, don't even begin to think of long-range planning, and don't concern yourself about the exercise schedule ahead. Get moving today, select an activity that appeals most to you personally, and enjoy it.

Bicycling is excellent exercise when you pump vigorously and steadily. If you just coast along, you're not doing your body much good. Enjoy the feeling of pumping with meaning and energy, and savor the outdoors and nature's beauties on a country road, a suburban lane, or a city park. Pumping hard in a spurt until you're breathless, and then coasting, is not best for using up calories and trimming off inches. Instead, pump and move along steadily at a good pace for 15 minutes or more each day (weather permitting, of course). You'll soon see the results.

Other activities that consume calories and firm the figure include badminton . . . handball (indoors and outdoors) . . . rowing . . . skating (on wheels and on ice) . . . skiing (on water and on snow) . . . squash . . . table tennis . . . tennis . . . and other sports you may enjoy. As long as you "put your body into it," and keep on steadily for 15 minutes or more, you're helping to speed up the slimming process as you drop pounds and inches through the Quick Teenage Diet.

Team sports are helpful, too, if they require steady exertion in using your body, moving your arms and legs, not in spurts and spasms, but fairly continuously. If you're not a competitive person, you'll probably prefer walking, swimming, or bicycling. When you're slimmed down, and that means having more vigor, vitality, and gracefulness of movement, then you may prefer to participate in team sports.

Judge the sports and activities that may provide relaxation but little exertion—that is, enjoy them, but don't count on the activity to use up calories or firm any flab. Such sports as archery, fishing, and sailing are fine for mental relaxation and pleasure, but—*in addition*—don't forget your daily exercise.

Personal Slimming-Trimming Exercises

Using the body in motion can provide exhilaration and enjoyment as well as calorie-cutting benefits if you approach exercising with a positive, rather than negative attitude. Unfortunately, many teenagers (and adults) are put off by the word "calisthenics" because they connect it with tedious, boring routine. Actually, calisthenics merely means "simple gymnastic exercises designed to develop muscular tone and to promote physical well-being . . . to gain grace of form and movement."

You don't have to be a gymnast, or perform calisthenics in a gymnasium, to get the most good from simple, private exercising. All alone, in your room or wherever you please, you can exercise your body as you wish, when you choose, consciously enjoying the knowledge that you are trimming fat and flab away through *action*. Just keep up your private exercising (if this is the form you choose) 15 minutes or more daily.

Use television, radio, or records, if you like, to make

your daily quarter-hour exercise period pass swiftly and enjoyably. Many excellent exercises can be performed standing or sitting, moving your arms, legs, body, without moving your eyes—so you can watch a television program for 15 minutes or a half-hour as you go through your slimming exertions. Or, with any exercises—bending, on your stomach or back, in any position—you can enlist radio programs and music to keep the beat and help keep you exercising.

Choose your exercises from newspaper and magazine articles, exercise books, school literature—the many sources that provide hundreds of different routines for your personal selection. Here are some slimming-trimming exercises to get you started; mix them up, add others—keep at it at least a quarter-hour per day:

1. MERRY-GO-ROUND: Stand relaxed but erect, your feet about 12" apart. Raise your arms straight up above your head. Keeping your arms in that position, bend from the hips and move your upper body with your arms in a wide circle to the right side, then front, then to left side, then erect again—to a slow count of 6.

Now, standing erect in original position, take a deep breath with your mouth open, to a slow count of 3, then expel.

Repeat the bending, circling from right to left. Then stop for a deep breath to count of 3. Repeat this bending, circling, breathing, 5 times from right to left.

Continuing, but this time bending and circling from *left to right,* repeat the left-to-right bending, circling, breathing—5 times, for a total of 10 times performing this "merry-go-round" exercise.

2. DOUBLE-UP: Lie flat on your back (on floor, bed, grass, any flat surface), legs outstretched straight ahead, arms close to body at sides. Now, to a slow count of 5, bend your knees and bring them up as close to your abdomen as possible *without straining,* while at the same time you lift your arms straight up, and back as far as possible. Then return slowly to original position.

156

Relax in that position on your back, and with mouth open breathe in deeply to a slow count of 3, then exhale.

Repeat the entire exercise 10 times.

3. *WHIRLWIND:* Stand erect with your feet 12″ to 18″ apart in a solid, comfortable stance. Now bend your knees slightly so that you're in a half-squatting position. Raise your arms straight in front of you, not stiff but comfortable, hands hanging limp.

Now, swing your body and arms slowly as far as possible to the right (without straining), then whirl slowly to the left as far as possible, then to right, then to left, and so on—completing the full right-to-left, then left-to-right, motions 20 times.

4. *SHOULDER-SHUDDER:* Stand erect, hands on hips. Bend your right knee and bring it as close as possible to your body (without straining) and, at the same time, keeping hands on hips, push your arms and shoulders back and try to make your shoulder blades touch. Hold that knee up, shoulders back, for a slow count of 3 —then return to original position, standing erect, hands on hips.

Repeat the exercise with your right knee 5 times, then with your left knee 5 times; then right knee 5 times, left knee 5 times—for a total of 20 times.

5. *FLAP-KICK:* Stand erect, arms and hands stiff at sides, your back against the wall for support. Now, keeping your right leg stiff, raise it straight ahead, as high as possible (without straining), and at the same time raise your stiff arms and hands at your sides to shoulder height. Keeping that position—leg raised straight ahead, arms raised at sides—take a deep breath with your mouth open, to a slow count of 3, then expel and return arms and leg slowly to your original position.

Repeat this "flap-kick" with your right leg 5 times, then with your left leg 5 times; then right leg 5 times, left leg 5 times—for a total of 20 times.

6. *MULE-KICK:* Place the palms of your hands flat on a table, desk, back of a heavy armchair, or other strong

support—standing a few inches away and bending slightly so that your weight rests primarily on the palms of your hands. Now slowly bend your right knee, then straighten your leg and kick back as far as possible (without straining); hold that position as you take a deep breath through your open mouth to a slow count of 3, then expel; bend your knee again and return to original position with your weight resting on the palms of your hands on table.

Now repeat the same knee-bending, leg-kicking, deep-breathing exercise with your left leg. Keep going, alternating right and left legs, for a total of 20 times—10 times with each leg.

Repeat all these exercises, or add other exercises of your choice, for a total workout of 15 minutes or more each day.

Using Mechanical Exercisers

Mechanical exercisers such as a stationary bicycle (motorized or not) . . . a rowing machine . . . walking-jogging platform . . . are excellent if they promote steady movement of your arms, legs, and body. Each exercise session should last 15 minutes or longer every day.

Teenagers using a TV set as an aid have trimmed and slimmed wonderfully with such exercisers in preference to other forms of exercise. For example, you can place a stationary bicycle (such exercisers are now available in a wide range of models and prices) a comfortable distance from the TV set and pump away steadily as you watch a half-hour program—your eyes fixed on the screen. The half-hour is over before you realize it, and you've had an excellent exercise session as long as you've worked at it, moving your body and limbs purposefully.

But don't count on "passive" items such as vibrating machines to take off ounces as well as inches—they simply don't work well in consuming calories. To burn up calories effectively, you must participate, using your arms, legs, torso energetically—in exercise, sports, or hard physical work (yes, scrubbing a floor energetically is a calorie-burning form of exertion).

Having a vibrating machine, or a belt, or having someone massage you as you just lie there, can be pleasurable (as one doctor puts it, "If you like having your flesh pushed around"), but the slimming-trimming effect is practically nil. The same is true of steam baths, sauna baths, other hot (or cold) treatments—they cause you to lose some perspiration through heat, or to shiver through cold, but cannot be counted on for any real weight loss or figure-trimming.

In short, you must use your body personally, move your arms, legs, and torso yourself, if you wish to burn calories and lose inches. Of course, you can enjoy massage, sauna baths, and so on, but don't ever let them replace real activity and swift reducing through the Quick Teenage Diet.

Extra Tips for Your Exercise/Activity Program

❋ *Drink lots of water* after you exercise, along with bouillon or broth, and no-calorie sodas. If you've been perspiring heavily, add some salt to the broth in order to help replace salt loss (better than salt tablets, which may upset your stomach).

❋ *Stop if you feel weak or exhausted.* It's better to rest a few moments, then use the QTD Oxygen Exercise, and continue, if you've only exercised for a few minutes. Or, if you're near the end of your exercise session, quit or finish up with a brisk walk.

❋ *Work up to full exercising gradually,* if necessary. If instructions advise "do it 20 times," and you're getting exhausted after 10 times, stop. The next day you can do the exercise 12 times . . . then 15 times . . . increasing day by day until you're up to the 20 times specified.

✻ *Wait about an hour* after a meal, a half-hour after a snack, before exercising energetically or engaging in active sports. Your circulatory system is busy after meals helping your stomach digest food properly, and should not be required to supply extra blood to exercising muscles at the same time. Walking normally, or engaging in the kind of work that doesn't require strenuous muscular action, can be done soon after eating.

✻ *Don't engage in strenuous activity* on an excessively hot day (okay in an air-conditioned interior). As always, just use your common sense. Don't overexert on weekends and then loll around all week. Pace yourself with adequate exercise and activity each day.

✻ *Enjoy a lukewarm shower or bath* after your exercise session, to cleanse your skin and help body temperature return to normal gradually. Don't shock your system with an icy shower or a plunge into cold water (better to walk in and cool yourself gradually at any time). An excessively hot shower or bath prolongs sweating and keeps your higher body temperature from coming down naturally to normal.

✻ *Try to get exercise daily,* indoors or outdoors. If your choice is brisk walking, and the weather is stormy, substitute an indoor exercise session instead. Mostly, keep active as much as possible at all times—don't lie around and get upset with yourself for not being up and about. Take a tip from the Greek philosopher Plato, who wrote over 1,500 years ago: "Exercise would almost cure a guilty conscience."

"Good Beginning Maketh Good Ending"

There's much wasteful controversy in trying to decide whether an overweight teenager gets heavy through lack of exercise—or whether he or she avoids exercise because of being heavy. That's a pointless puzzlement, as frustrating as the old question, "Which came first, the chicken or the egg?" Whatever may have kept you from exercising your body enough, the important step is to begin exercising today. Then get your exercise and keep active each day, one day at a time.

Keep in mind as you slim down that, "One day, with life and heart, is more than enough to find a world." For you, that means at least in part a better world ahead where you are trimmer and healthier. Slimmed down, you'll be more eager and able to participate, to do the things that feed your mind and spirit best (rather than your stomach). That's a personal world worth working toward—*actively*.

11

Keep-Slim Eating for the Rest of Your Happier Life

A pretty teenage patient who had slimmed down a great deal on the Quick Teenage Diet told me that she had gained much more than she had lost. "I lost 30 pounds," she said, "but I gained 100 pounds in self-respect!" She added, "I know that I'll keep slim, I'll never get fat again. Now that I've reached my goal, I'm convinced once and for all that it can be done—by me—and I know the way to do it for the rest of my life. I'll never lose my slender figure or my self-respect again. I've discovered, and I'll never forget it, that my figure and my health and feeling of well-being are far more important than my stomach."

One of the most valuable things you will have learned while dieting is that *"eating," as such, is one of the least important things in living*. I cannot emphasize this too much; as I stressed repeatedly in the past to overweight teenagers in my office, eating is only a means to the goal of living vigorously and healthfully. The way to achieve that is through controlled eating, not overeating that fattens and defeats you.

You will have seen for yourself, once you start QTD eating, that an ounce of restraint is worth a pound of fat. As the habit of eating less, of eating lower-calorie meals, becomes second nature to you, you will find that "habit is stronger than nature." I have seen overweight teenagers, who claimed that it was their "nature" to overeat, change as they finally slimmed down—and they never went back to overeating as long as I knew them.

Once and for all, you can dismiss the idea that you

163

were "born to be fat" (a controversial subject in medical science). Such excuses are futile. As I've emphasized a number of times, if your metabolism is off, for instance, your doctor will know it upon examination and will act to correct the condition. Since fewer than 5 percent of overweight teenagers have a faulty metabolism, you must realize that chances are 20 to 1 (probably closer to 50 to 1) against your being overweight because of anything but overeating.

Happily for you, with the Quick Teenage Diet you have a means for not only getting slim, but keeping slim. This rapid-reducing method is a handy tool that can serve you again and again. Use it in combination with Keep-Slim Eating as instructed in this chapter. If your weight sneaks up on you, take off the excess in a few days by returning to the Quick Teenage Diet. If you put on weight over a party weekend, or a vacation or holiday, take it off immediately by returning to the Quick Teenage Diet until you're at your desired weight again.

With some people, weight is like the tide—it comes in and it goes out. Don't worry about such ups and downs; instead, do something about it. If you go up, you can bring it down quickly and surely, and you're no worse off for the temporary increase in poundage. Just get slim and you can keep slim from now on.

Your Next Step: Keep Slim

Once you are at your desired weight, you can learn the Keep-Slim way of eating. With Keep-Slim, you eat what you like best, limiting the daily quantities and calories. You stay away almost completely from the extra-rich, extra-fattening foods (perhaps indulging occasionally), but you don't feel at all deprived. In fact, you're likely to find that while on the Quick Teenage Diet, you come to dislike the "greasy, over-rich taste" of high-calorie foods. Chances are that you actually will prefer fresh natural flavors, without heavy, high-calorie additives. That's the case with so many ex-heavyweight QTD dieters.

The basic reason for being able to resist is that you will have achieved a marvelous new realization. In exchange for giving up some high-calorie "taste treats," you are more than compensated by having a more attractive figure—*and you are no longer deprived of activities denied you while you were fat!* You can play, dance, participate in sports and social pleasures along with others. You have shed the drag and burden, physical and emotional, of bulges and layers of fat that hampered your free movement and energetic health.

Deprived by giving up high-calorie, rich, fattening foods? Exactly the opposite! You realize exultantly that, newly slim, you never enjoyed life so much.

Keep-Slim Basis: Calories DO Count

You didn't have to count calories on the Quick Teenage Diet because you ate from a selection of all-protein foods (plus skim milk). As discussed earlier, you have the advantage on that diet of eating foods that burn calories with a "higher flame." On Keep-Slim Eating you just must be sure not to eat more calories than you burn.

Controlling your calorie intake is as clear as comparing these two breakfasts:

Fat-Producing Breakfast:
　　8 oz. of orange juice
　　2 scrambled eggs in butter
　　2 slices of toast with butter
　　1 glass of whole milk
　　Coffee with sugar and cream
　　　　　　　　TOTAL: over 900 calories

Keep-Slim Breakfast:
　　4 oz. of tomato juice
　　4 tablespoons of creamed cottage cheese

1 slice of toast (thin-sliced preferably)
4 oz. of skim milk
1 vitamin-mineral tablet

TOTAL: about 200 calories

This, in Keep-Slim Eating, enjoying the Keep-Slim Breakfast, with its plentiful food values and bulk, compared with the Fat-Producing Breakfast (the kind of "hearty" breakfast urged on teenagers by too many people), *saves you 700 calories*. This kind of calorie-counting makes the basic difference between putting on pounds or staying at your ideal weight.

From now on, don't you ever believe anyone who tells you that excessive calories are "good for you." To the contrary, *excessive calories can kill you* as surely as they kill your good looks. Don't let anyone ever mislead you with the false statement that "fat melts away fat." That's absolutely untrue—added fat does just the opposite, it adds to your weight.

Keep those calories down, and you keep your weight down—it's as basic as that, once you are down at your desired weight (adjusting somewhat year by year according to your age and height until you have reached your full growth). In short, Keep-Slim Eating is as clear and simple as this 1–2 guide:

1. Figure your daily calorie intake to stay at ideal weight. Look back at the weight charts in Chapter 2 . . . to check again your ideal and desired weight for your age and height. Then, recheck again here how to maintain your ideal or desired weight (as you choose):

Females—multiply each pound of total weight by 12 to arrive at approximately the number of calories per day that will keep you at that weight. If your desired weight is 110 lbs., multiply 110 x 12, for a total in this case of 1,300–1,350 calories per day to keep at that weight.

Males—multiply each pound of total desired weight by 13 to arrive at approximately the number of calories per day that will keep you at that weight. If your desired weight is 140 lbs., multiply 140 x 13, for a total of 1,800–1,850 calories per day to keep you at that weight.

Everyone, female or male, is different to some degree, so if you find that you are gaining at the figured calorie count for your desired weight, reduce your calorie intake a little. If losing weight, increase your calorie intake slightly, then a bit more, if necessary, until you arrive at the correct amount to maintain desired weight.

From now on, adjusting if necessary year by year, you will eat within the Keep-Slim calorie count. If you go over the calorie total considerably on any day, cut back accordingly the next day. It's the average that counts in keeping you slim.

Weighing yourself each morning upon arising will enable you to keep track of how you're doing. The great benefits you get from being slim are not just a reward, they're a *result* of keeping your calorie intake in control and checking up on yourself every day. That simple procedure is essential and certainly worth while.

2. *Count calories until it becomes second nature.* Consult the calorie chart at the end of this chapter (or any calorie chart—counts may vary slightly but are basically the same). A few calories variation, plus or minus, are not important in gaining or losing weight, but obviously a difference of *hundreds* of calories above your daily Keep-Slim total can pile on the pounds.

You'll find that after a week or less of calorie-counting, you will learn the calorie totals of most foods. When you consider what to eat, or look at a menu when eating out, your brain will soon tell you automatically that a 4-ounce glass of orange juice has 55 calories, a frankfurter has 150 calories plus 100 calories for a roll, an ice cream sundae has 300 calories or about 400 with whipped cream topping, and so on.

Take the attitude that calorie-counting is a game rather than a grind. When you get down to ideal weight, you'll be so proud of taking off the fat, and so pleased not to be an overweight, that you won't be at all embarrassed

167

about counting calories even in front of others. However, you can keep it to yourself if you wish; it's your own decision entirely. Many teenagers I know say that they have fun counting calories as in doing a crossword puzzle or solving other challenging puzzles.

On Keep-Slim Eating, you can choose what you eat, as you wish, staying with lower-calorie foods most of the time. For example, here's a typical healthful day of eating for a teenager whose Keep-Slim total is 1,300–1,350 daily:

BREAKFAST

1 vitamin-mineral tablet	
4 oz. orange juice	55 cal.
1 slice whole wheat toast with artificially sweetened jam or jelly	60
1 silce whole wheat tosat with artificially	
1 glass skim milk	90
	205

LUNCH

4 oz. tomato juice	25
4 oz. broiled hamburger with pickle relish on roll	350
1 serving regular gelatin dessert	80
Artifically sweetened "no-calorie" soda	5
	460

DINNER

1 cup chicken consommé (fat removed)	10
6 oz. broiled chicken	300
6 medium asparagus stalks	20
1 cup wax beans	30

Lettuce and tomato salad with low-calorie	
salad dressing	25
Angel food cake, medium portion	150
1 glass skim milk	90

625

Total for day: 1,290 calories

In that 1,300-calorie day of eating, you can see that you'll be getting lots of delicious, healthful food. By calorie-counting, you can vary the selections to suit your personal wishes in almost infinite variety. Here's an example of one substitution:

> *Instead of angel cake for dinner,* you could skip dessert or have a serving of artificially sweetened gelatin dessert, saving about 150 calories.

> *You could then substitute as snacks* during the day, or extras at meals, any of these or other selections of your own from the calorie tables:

> ... 1 medium raw apple (80) and 2 medium peaches (35 each)

> ... or a medium-size sliced orange (75) and a cup of diced pineapple (no-sugar syrup) (75 calories)

> ... or a cup of fresh strawberries (60) and 2 plums (35 each)

It's that simple to figure out your daily total from the calorie tables on Keep-Slim Eating. It's that easy to keep your slim figure, not only in these important teenage years, but for the rest of your life. You can take immediate and enduring pleasure in caring about your appearance and health—instead of being a glutton, a depressed victim of "hand-to-mouth disease."

If You Want to Splurge

"The only way to get rid of a temptation," Oscar Wilde quipped, "is to yield to it." If you must yield to temptation once in a while, there's no harm done on Keep-Slim Eating as long as you count your calories correctly, and stay within your Keep-Slim daily limit. It's a cinch to hold your weight down even if you splurge on an ice cream soda, for example.

Instead of the 460-calorie lunch on the 1,300-calorie day just listed, you could skip those foods and instead eat:

2 hard-boiled eggs	....	150 calories
Ice cream soda	....	300

450 total calories

It's up to you. I suggest that you don't get into the habit of yielding to temptation, as no one knows better than you will (as an ex-overweight) how the calories and pounds and inches can pile on disgustingly. But giving yourself occasional "treats"—*within your Keep-Slim calorie total*—won't push you over your desired weight. Don't feel any pangs of guilt, or fear that you're spoiling your good health, when you indulge your temptations now and then.

Beware of Fat-Producing High-Calorie Eating!

No matter how many enticing recipes you come across, or TV commercials or other ads urging you to indulge in heavy breakfasts such as griddle cakes and syrup and butter, *you keep counting calories.* Your personal concerns are your good looks and your good health, not the profits or misguided advice of those who urge you in effect to pile on the fat.

If you don't keep track of your daily intake, if you don't count your calories on Keep-Slim Eating, you can gain weight so fast that it can actually make your head spin. For instance, how many calories do you think you'd consume in a single day of fat-producing overeating like the following (without adding a solitary snack during the day)?

Typical Get-Fatter Overeating Day

Breakfast

1 6-oz. glass orange juice	90 cal.
3 griddle cakes with syrup and butter..	950
3 small pork sausages	150
1 glass whole milk	170

1,360

Lunch

1 cup bean soup	175
2 frankfurters on rolls	400
1 portion french-fried potatoes	200
Chocolate cake with icing	400
1 8-oz. glass regular soda	100

1,275

Dinner

1 cup fruit cocktail with syrup	150
6-oz. meat loaf	300
1 cup baked beans	330
1 cup mashed potatoes	200
1 roll with butter	150
1 medium slice apple pie	200
1 glass whole milk	170

1,400

Total calories get-fatter overeating day: 4,935
That total is enough to make you sick—as it does so many overweight teenagers who don't realize how many

excess calories they're stuffing into themselves. Imagine eating close to 5,000 calories per day, when your Keep-Slim calorie count indicates 1,300–1,350. That's almost four times as many calories as specified for keeping you at your desired slim, trim weight and figure! Just *one* of those get-fatter, overeating meals had about *a full day's calories* for keeping slim at this teenager's age and height.

Don't let anyone tell you that this calorie count for a typical get-fatter, overeating day is exaggerated. Notice that *hundreds* of hidden calories have been left out of this counted day that might normally be eaten by the overweight. I haven't counted in the "hidden calories" of heavy gravies, second helpings at meals, 2 or 3 rolls with dinner instead of the single roll listed, snacks all day and evening of candies, cakes, cookies, and ice cream.

Check Calories by Category

An easy way to plan your day's calories (or in choosing items to eat in the school lunchroom or eating out anywhere), is to get to know the calorie counts of different categories of the same foods. In selecting vegetables, for example, or discussing what meals are to be prepared at home, you can save more calories for other foods if you choose two of the *lower*-calorie vegetables. Or, you can have one higher-calorie vegetable of your preference instead of two vegetables that total the same number of calories.

It's easy to count vegetable calories when grouped this way (these are 1-cup portions, which are generous servings; to cut calories in half, just take the equivalent of a ½-cup serving which you may consider sufficient to accompany other foods at the meal):

25–35 calories per cup (or general equivalent): asparagus . . . green beans . . . wax beans . . . cabbage, raw or boiled . . . carrots, raw . . . cauliflower . . . celery . . . cucumber . . . lettuce . . . okra . . . peppers . . . pickles

. . . radishes . . . sauerkraut . . . summer squash . . . tomato.

36–55 calories (or general equivalent): beets . . . broccoli . . . brussels sprouts . . . cooked carrots . . . mushrooms . . . onion . . . popcorn (no butter) . . . spinach . . . zucchini.

Over 60 calories per cup (up to 450 for hash-browned potatoes): avocado (250) . . . baked beans (325) . . . lima beans (175) . . . corn (140) . . . parsnips (100) . . . potatoes (from 1 small boiled potato (65) to 1 small baked potato (95) to mashed potatoes (185, without butter) to fried potatoes (200–450 calories).

You can choose similarly in other categories—fruits, meats, and so on.

Save Calories with Low-Calorie Prepared Food

Check into and take advantage of the increasing number of low-calorie products you can get today. Whenever you can substitute a low-calorie equivalent for a higher-calorie brand of the same food or beverage, you can increase your intake of other wanted foods. For instance, by having an 8-oz. glass of "no-calorie" artificially sweetened soda instead of regular soda made with sugar, you save close to a hundred calories. Therefore, by the savings on the soda substitute, you could add an egg (75) and a nectarine (30) to your daily meals or snacks—or any foods totaling about 100 calories.

Taking just a few of the available low-calorie "substitutes" which you might use in a day's eating, see how many calories you would save:

Regular Food	LOW-CALORIE SUBSTITUTE
2 glasses whole milk 340	2 gl. skim milk 180
1 slice bread 70	2 pcs. melba toast 30
1 oz. regular jam 75	1 oz. art. sw. jam 10
2 pats butter 100	Skip butter or marg. .. 0
1 tbsp. mayonnaise 100	1 tbsp. imit. mayon. 20
1 tbsp. salad dressing .. 70	1 tbsp. low-cal. dressg. 15
2 8-oz. gl. reg. soda 200	2 8-oz. "no-cal." soda .. 10
955	265

On the preceding listing alone, simply by substituting the low-calorie equivalents for the same few items, you would save nearly *700 calories*. That's about half as many calories as your total if your Keep-Slim daily maintenance figure for your age and height is 1,300–1,350 calories.

It certainly pays to use the low-calorie foods available. In sodas, for example, blindfold tests prove that most teenagers can't tell any difference in taste between artificially sweetened sodas and those made with sugar. It's worth repeating here—check the label for the *number of calories* in the brand, since some items such as sodas marked "low-calorie" on the label are actually fairly high in total calories. Trust the fine print on the label only.

Don't believe claims on food labels such as "Diet Margarine" (or other foods labeled "Diet"), or "Low Calorie," or "Reduced-in-Calories," or any other such possible "permissible lie" (considered "permissible" by the maker because he thinks it increases his sales and profits). For instance, one brand of regular margarine is 100 calories for just 1 tablespoon; the "diet margarine" of the same brand is 50 calories for 1 tablespoon, still a lot of calories for that small amount of margarine.

Many low-calorie claims are "fat lies"—don't let yourself be deceived. Realize, as just one small example, that only 1 tablespoon of "diet margarine" (50 calories) melted on 6 medium-size spears of asparagus (20 calories) *adds 2½ times as many calories as are in the asparagus alone!*

Keep-Slim Eating Checkpoints

❊ *Have a vitamin-mineral tablet daily* on Keep-Slim Eating, as during your dieting. I prefer that you get the extra vitamins and minerals every day as a teenager, since they won't do you any harm, and may do some good, as long as you only take the recommended amount.

❊ *Include plenty of proteins* in the Keep-Slim meals of your choice. Meat, poultry, fish, shellfish (unless you have acne), eggs, and cottage cheese—along with vegetables and fruits—are the healthful basics for Keep-Slim Eating for the rest of your life.

❊ *Drink 6 glasses of water* or more per day. This is one of the most healthful habits you can develop, no matter what or how you eat. The flow of water, plus other beverages, helps keep you slim, too, by washing out waste matter. Drinking lots of water is excellent for your general good health, and an aid in having a clear, attractive skin. That holds true through your adult years, too.

❊ *Don't overlook "concealed calories"* in figuring how many calories you consume per day on Keep-Slim Eating. Such hidden calories as butter used on vegetables when cooking, an occasional candy and cooky as a snack, all mount up during the day's eating. Rich, heavy gravies, sauces, and dressings can add *hundreds of calories* to a dish of meat and other foods. Skip the sauce, and you skip loads of fattening calories.

❊ *BEWARE the "3-Pound-Warning"* on your bathroom scale. Some of my teenage patients have taped to the bathroom scale a card with desired weight lettered large—bigger than the numbers on the scale. Keep your desired weight number in sight or in mind. Any time the scale shows 3 pounds over that figure, go right back on the Quick Teenage Diet for a few days until you're back at your desired weight again. If you return from a heavy weekend away, or from a big-eating vacation, use the numbers on the scale to springboard you right back to one of my diets. QTD is your ready aide at all times when your weight tends to go up.

* *Cut your calorie total intake* if you are gaining weight on the Keep-Slim number of calories you have figured out to be your daily allowance. If your number is 1,300 calories per day, for example, cut to 1,250, or whatever total you find keeps you at your desired weight. As I have stated, no two individuals are alike, so you must arrive at your own lucky Keep-Slim number by trial and adjustment.

* *Keep active and exercise* every possible day. The more you exercise, the more calories you use up. As a general guide, here are some figures on how many calories certain activities use up (numbers cannot be precise because of differences in size, pace, and other variables); these figures are calculated on a half-hour of activity for a person weighing 125 lbs. (remember, the numbers are necessarily very approximate):

Bicycling	200-250 cal. per ½ hr.
Bowling	75-100
Dancing vigorously	125-175
Driving auto	25-40
Gardening vigorously	100-150
Golf	75-100
Handball (indoors, outdoors)	150-250
Horseback riding	100-200
Housework, vigorous	75-150
Jogging	200-250
Lying around	20-30
Rowing	200-250
Running	300-400
Sitting	30-40
Skating (ice, roller)	150-200
Skiing (snow, water)	200-250

Squash (indoors, outdoors) 200-250
Standing relaxed 25-40
Swimming vigorously 200-250
Table tennis 125-175
Tennis 150-250
Typing, desk work 30-60
Volleyball 75-100
Walking briskly 75-150

Calories used per half-hour in team sports are difficult to calculate because of the amount of activity involved in the position you play in the particular sport. Judge for yourself according to the comparable amount of motion in other activities in the preceding listing.

If you like to play around with numbers, it may interest you that 1 pound of body fat roughly equals 3,500 calories. Thus, if you bicycle at 200 calories per half-hour (400 per hour), you would use up 1 pound of fat about every 9 days, if you were to bicycle about an hour a day.

❋ *Spread your daily eating* over 5 or 6 meals a day instead of the usual 3 meals, and you'll slim down further or be able to keep slim while eating 100–200 more calories per day. As advised elsewhere, while the scientific reason isn't clear, the fact is that you can eat 1,400–1,450 calories a day in 6 meals, compared with 1,300–1,350 calories in 3 meals a day—and stay the same weight.

❋ *Don't ever overload at any single meal!* You can skip a meal without any harm at all, but don't pile in a mass of food at a time, since this is very dangerous to your health. It's like overloading a wheelbarrow to the point where it breaks down. This can happen to the human body as well.

❋ *Vegetables and salads are great helps* in Keep-Slim Eating. You can load up your plate with lots of the lower-calorie vegetables and salad greens, without loading up on calories. Avoid adding butter, margarine, and rich dressings, of course. Add cottage cheese or a hard-boiled egg for protein.

❋ *Keep low-calorie snacks handy* in the refrigerator.

You can munch on carrot sticks, radishes, raw cauliflower, celery, lettuce, small tomatoes—without consuming many calories. Small peaches, plums, apples, tangerines—all make tasty snacks without adding many calories (unless you eat too many, of course).

✻ *Keep handy in the refrigerator* servings of artificially sweetened gelatin desserts in a variety of flavors—comparatively few calories per serving.

✻ *In seconds, you can mix up* a bracing, filling cup of chicken, beef, vegetable, or other consommé, broth, or bouillon, with hot water and fat-free cubes, powder, or liquid concentrate.

✻ *"No-calorie" artificially sweetened sodas,* coffee and tea if part of your normal eating (skip the cream and sugar, add artificial sweetening and a dash of skim milk or powdered non-dairy creamer, if wanted), are refreshing and filling without piling on unwanted calories.

✻ *Food seems more filling* when you cut it in small pieces, eat and chew slowly. Benefit from the horrible example of a terribly bulky California teenager—an acquaintance said, "She has the fastest gums in the West!"

✻ *Eating slowly is excellent* to appease the brain and the stomach, while gulping food is far less satisfying. Also, chewing is good for the gums. Cut even an apple or pear into small chunks, and chew slowly.

✻ *Stay away from butter, margarine, oils, fats* of all kinds as much as possible. When doing your own cooking (or discuss with the person doing the cooking), use non-stick pans that don't require any fats. For instance, you don't need butter to scramble eggs in a non-stick pan; add a dash of skim milk, herbs and spices, beat up the eggs, and they're delicious without the extra calories of any cooking fats.

✻ *Don't be fooled by foods labeled "fat-free,"* such as some brands of milk and cottage cheese. Instead of animal "fats," these products usually contain added vegetable oils, which are almost as high in calories as animal fats—and are, in effect, "fats" themselves.

❋ *Cut away every bit of visible fat* on the foods you eat. Remove the skin from chicken. Trim off the fat from the steak or other meat on your plate. When ground beef is purchased for hamburgers, ask that the butcher trim off all visible fat before grinding the beef—that removes many calories.

❋ *Avoid fat-fried foods as much as possible.* Broiling, roasting, and boiling, skimming off the fat while cooking, not only keep the calories down but make foods much healthier and easier to digest.

❋ *Don't eat or snack while watching TV,* listening to music, watching movies, just chatting with others, and so on. What usually happens in such cases is that you keep stuffing food into your mouth without even realizing it. You might finish off a dish of peanuts or potato chips before you stopped and figured out how many *hundreds* of extra fat-producing calories you were consuming. Be aware of what you eat every minute, and keep the total calories within your daily Keep-Slim limit.

❋ *Never forget that self-discipline* in Keep-Slim Eating pays off in a slimmer figure, a far greater reward than any temporary pleasure from stuffing food into your stomach. If someone fills your plate with too much high-calorie food, *don't eat it all.* If required by "politeness," nibble at the food, push it around with your fork as though eating, keep talking instead of eating, until the plate is removed with most of the food left on it. Don't feel self-conscious—so many teenagers today are weight-conscious that you're not unique or alone.

❋ *Don't take it for granted* that a food is low in calories because you "think" so, or others tell you so. They may be honestly mistaken or wish to mislead you deliberately for their own reasons. *Look up the food in the calorie tables and make sure!* The number of calories in foods is what counts, not the weight of the food itself. For example, ¼ lb. of butter or margarine has about 1,800

179

calories—while 14 lbs. of selected lower-calorie vegetables have only about 900 calories.

Most people think that ice milk and sherbert are much lower in calories than ice cream, half the calories or even fewer, but here are the facts supplied by a leading manufacturer of such products. These figures are for 4 fluid ounces or ¼ pint, a moderate portion:

Ice cream (16½% butterfat) 225 cal. (incl. chocolate)
Ice milk (5% butterfat) 135
Sherbet 136
"Dietetic Ice Cream" 145

While you save some calories when substituting ice milk, sherbet, or "dietetic ice cream" for regular ice cream, a moderate portion of any of them is still well over 100 calories, not exactly "low in calories." You can eat them, within your daily Keep-Slim total, *but know the correct calorie numbers.*

✳ *When you are full, stop eating.* Don't hesitate to leave food on your plate (may be saved for a snack or the next meal). When you're eating at someone's home, ask for small portions. It's not impolite to say that you're watching your weight and therefore limiting the amount and the kinds of food you eat.

Many a world-famous gourmet stays slim by sampling instead of stuffing with delicious foods (that's a tip from one of the leading food editors, as well as from me). Any hostess or friend who resents your not stuffing yourself as a mealtime guest is not being a "friend" in caring about your personal well-being.

✳ *Double-check sizes of portions—it's easy.* "A glass" or "a measuring cup" means 8 ounces, so use a marked measuring cup to check how many ounces fill the glass you usually use, since glasses can hold from 6 ounces to 12 ounces. A small "orange juice glass" is generally 4 ounces, so fill it only halfway for 2 ounces of juice. For 4 ounces of cottage cheese (or other food), scoop out half of an 8-ounce package (contents printed on outside). For 4 ounces of hamburger, use a fourth of a 1-pound package. Soon you'll be able to recognize the approximate portions wanted without measuring.

✳ *Keep busy, active, and involved in many things.* It has proved true repeatedly that "the happy people are those who are producing something; the bored people are those who are consuming much and producing nothing." Fill your mind and your hours with interesting knowledge and pursuits, and you'll be far less likely to fill your stomach with fattening foods. Keeping slim, for the ex-overweight, is a vital aid in keeping happy—so never let down. People will respect your new figure and your new outlook.

KEEP-SLIM CALORIE TABLES

While calorie counts are exact measurements, there are some slight variations in tables due to differences in sizes (as in an orange), amount on a tablespoon, and so on. Such small differences are not important—it's the total calories per day that count. The following table may be used as your basic guide for Keep-Slim Eating.

MEATS AND POULTRY   cals.

(Most meats and poultry figured here as lean, all visible fat trimmed off, about 60 calories per ounce.)

	cals.
Bacon, fried crisp, 2 slices	95
Beef roast, lean, 4 oz.	210
Hamburger, lean, broiled, 4 oz.	245
Potpie, 8 oz.	460
Steak, lean, broiled, 4 oz.	235
Bologna, 4″ slice	85
Chicken, turkey, broiled, 3 oz.	180
Drumstick and thigh with bone, fried, 5 oz.	275
Frankfurter, medium	155
Ham, smoked, 3 oz.	290
Canned, all lean, 2 oz.	170
Lamb chop, broiled, lean only, 2.5 oz.	140
Leg, lean, 2.5 oz.	130

Pork roast, lean only,
2.5 oz. 175
Sausage, 4 oz. 340
Tongue, beef, 3 oz. 205
Veal cutlet, broiled,
3 oz. 185
Roast, lean, 3 oz. 280

FISH AND SHELLFISH

Bluefish, baked,
broiled, 3 oz. 135
Clams, medium,
each 9
Crabmeat, 3 oz. 90
Haddock, fried, 3 oz. .. 135
Mackerel, broiled,
3 oz. 200
Oysters, medium,
each 12
Salmon, canned,
drained, 3 oz. 120
Sardines, canned,
drained, 3 oz. 180
Shad, baked, 3 oz. 170
Shrimps, medium,
each 10
Swordfish, broiled
with butter, 3 oz. 150
Tuna, canned,
drained, 3 oz. 170

VEGETABLES

Asparagus, med. 3.5
Avocado, medium,
half 185

Beans, baked and
canned types,
1 cup 320
Beets, 1 cup 70
Broccoli, 1 cup 45
Brussels sprouts,
1 cup 60
Cabbage, raw,
shredded, 1 cup 25
Cooked, 1 cup 45
Carrots, raw, 5½",
each 20
Cooked, 1 cup 45
Cauliflower, cooked,
1 cup 30
Celery, 8" stalk, raw .. 5
Corn, cooked, 5"
ear 65
Canned, 1 cup 170
Cucumbers, 7½",
each 25
Lettuce, 5" compact
head, 1 lb. 70
2 large leaves 5
Lima beans, 1 cup 150
Mushrooms, 1 cup 30
Onions, raw, 2½",
each 50
Cooked, 1 cup 80
Parsley, raw,
chopped, 1 tbsp. 1
Peas, fresh, cooked,
1 cup 110
Canned, frozen,
drained, 1 cup 80
Potatoes, medium,
baked, with peel,
each 105

without peel, each .. 90

Boiled, medium, each 90

French-fried 2" x ½", each 15

Mashed, milk, no butter, 1 cup 145

Chips, 2", medium, each 11

Radishes, raw, medium, each 3

Sauerkraut, drained, 1 cup 30

Spinach and other greens, 1 cup 45

Squash, summer type, 1 cup 35

Winter type, 1 cup .. 95

String beans, 1 cup 35

Sweet potatoes, medium, baked 155

Candied 295

Tomatoes, raw, med. .. 30

Canned, 1 cup 45

Juice, 1 cup (8 oz.) 50

FRUITS

Apples, raw, med. 70

Juice, 1 cup 125

Applesauce, can., sweetened, 1 cup 185

Apricots, raw, each 20

Canned in syrup, 1 cup 220

Bananas, med., ea. 85

Blueberries, black-

berries, 1 cup 85

Cantaloupe, 5", med. half 40

Cherries, 1 cup 65

Cranberry sauce, canned, 1 cup 550

Dates, pitted, 1 cup .. 505

Figs, dried, large 2" x 1", each 60

Fruit Cocktail, canned, in syrup, 1 cup 195

Grapefruit, 5" medium, half 55

Juice, fresh, 1 cup .. 95

Grapes, 1 cup 85

Grape juice, bottled, 1 cup 165

Lemons, medium, each 20

Oranges, medium, each 65

Juice, fresh, 1 cup .. 110

Peaches, 2" medium, each 35

Canned in syrup, pitted, 1 cup 200

Pears, 3" medium each 100

Pineapple, fresh, diced, 1 cup 75

Canned in syrup, 1 cup 205

Plums, 2" medium, each 30

Prunes, cooked, un-sweetened, each 17

Juice, can., 1 cup .. 170

Raisins, dried, 1 cup .. 460
  1 level tbsp. 30
Strawberries, fresh,
  1 cup 70
Tangerines, med.
  2½", each 40
Watermelon, 4" x 8"
  wedge 120

DAIRY PRODUCTS, EGGS, FATS, OILS, DRESSINGS

Butter, 1 8-oz. cup
  (2 ¼-lb. sticks) .. 1,605
  1 pat or square 50
Cheese, American,
  1-inch cube 70
  Amer., process,
    1 oz. 105
  Cottage cheese,
    creamed, 1 oz. 30
  Farmer cheese,
    pot cheese, 1 oz. .. 25
  Cream cheese, 1 oz. 105
  Roquefort-type,
    1 oz. 105
  Swiss, 1 oz. 105
Eggs, large, cooked
  without fat, each 80
  Scrambled, fried
    with butter, each 115
  White only, raw,
    each 20
  Yolk only, raw,
    each 60
Milk (cow's) whole,

1 cup (8 oz.) 165
Skim, nonfat, 1 cup 90
Buttermilk, cult.,
  1 cup 90
Cream, light, 1 cup 525
  "   1 tbsp. 35
  "   heavy,
      tbsp. 50
Margarine, 1 cup
  (2 ¼-lb. sticks) .. 1,615
  1 pat or square 50
Oils, cooking and
  salad—corn, cot-
  tonseed, olive,
  soybean, 1 tbsp. .. 125
Salad dressings—
  French, 1 tbsp. 60
  Mayonnaise, 1 tbsp. 110
  Mayonnaise-type,
    1 tbsp. 60
  Russian, 1 tbsp. 75
Yogurt, plain, 1 cup .. 120

BREADS AND GRAIN PRODUCTS

Bread, all types,
  average slice,
  plain, toasted 60
Cereals, cooked,
  average type, 1 c. .. 105
  Dry cereals, un-
  sweetened, aver.,
  1 oz. 110
Crackers, Graham,
  medium, each 28
Rye wafers, 2" x
  3½", each 25

Saltines, 2" square,
each 23

Macaroni, spaghetti,
cooked, 1 cup 155

Muffins, 3" size,
av., each 140

Noodles, egg,
cooked, 1 cup 200

Pancakes, 4", ea. 55

Rice, cooked, 1 cup 200

Rolls, med. size,
av., each 130

Waffles, av. size,
each 240

DESSERTS, SWEETS

Cakes, Angel food,
2" sector 110

Chocolate layer,
2" sector 420

Cupcake, 2¾",
with icing, ea. 160

Plain cake, 3" x 2"
x 1½", piece 180

Sponge cake, 2"
sector 115

Candy, Caramels,
fudge, 1 oz. 120

Chocolate, milk or
dark, 1 oz. 145

Cookies, Average
type, 3" round,
each 110

Fig bar, small, ea. .. 55

Chocolate syrup,
1 tbsp. 20

Doughnuts, med.,

plain, each 135

Gelatin dessert, ½
cup 80
sugar-free 10

Honey, 1 tbsp. 60

Ice cream, ½ cup 200
Ice cream soda,
average size 350
Ice milk, 1 cup 285

Jams, jellies, pre-
serves, 1 tbsp. 55

Pies, apple, other
fruits, 4" sector 330
Custard, pumpkin,
4" sector 265
Lemon meringue,
4" sector 300

Puddings, custard,
cornstarch, 1 cup 275

Sherbet, ices, ½ cup .. 120

Sugar, granulated,
1 tsp. 16

Sugar, granulated,
1 cup 770

Syrup, 1 tbsp. 55

MISCELLANEOUS

Beverages, Coffee,
tea, plain 0

Beer, 8 oz. 110
Cocktail, aver. 150
Gin, Scotch, vodka,
whiskey, aver.,
1 oz. 75

Carbonated bever-
ages, ginger ale,
8 oz. 80

Cola-type, 8 oz. 105

Cocoa, cup 235

Ketchup, chili sauce,
2 tbsp. 15

Olives, green and
ripe, large, each,
average 9

Nuts, Peanuts,
roasted, shelled,
½ cup 420

Peanut butter, 1
tbsp. 90

Cashews, pecans,
walnuts, ½ c. 375

Pickles, dill 4", sweet
3", each 18

Pizza, cheese, 6"
wedge 200

Soups, Bouillon,
broth, consommé,
1 cup 10

Chicken, tomato,
vegetable 80

Creamed, aspara-
gus, mushroom
1 cup 200

Rice, noodle,
barley, 1 cup 115

12

Quick, Easy Recipes for the Quick Teenage Diet

Here is a sampling of some recipes for the Quick Teenage Diet, to give you an idea of the dishes that you (or whoever prepares the meals in your home) can easily create. I recommend that you mostly eat simple broiled, baked, roasted, and boiled meats, chicken, turkey, fish, seafood, along with cottage cheese and eggs, simply prepared without any fuss or frills.

However, many people of all ages using my high-protein rapid-reducing methods have told me that they enjoy creating recipe variations with the basic foods listed. If you need inspiration, here are some basic recipes to start you off.

Most important in preparing servings for the Quick Teenage Diet, the "cook" must accept a new, very healthful challenge—to prepare foods without any butter, margarine, oils, mayonnaise, rich dressings, sauces, gravies, or any fats whatsoever. *This new way of cooking will provide slimming, life-saving, life-prolonging benefits not only for you, but for every member of the family.*

Soon you will discover all sorts of pleasing natural flavors and by eliminating the high-calorie fat additives, you avoid *hundreds* of calories per day and *thousands* of calories per week—an enormous help in slimming down swiftly and beautifully. For example, by frying an egg in a non-stick no-fat pan, instead of using a tablespoon of butter in the pan, *you save 100 calories!*

Enjoy the simple recipes which follow—and the fun of creating many more variations of your own with the basic

Quick Teenage Diet foods. Use the foods singly, or in pleasing, creative combinations. Many teenagers have enjoyed whipping up their own QTD concoctions; one bright girl wrote, "I've originated over 100 recipes myself!" (she reduced from 150 to 105 pounds, including her own recipes based on the permitted foods only).

Don't be fussy about slight variations in ingredients (use what you have handy in spices and seasonings) or types of permitted foods; for example, don't start worrying about whether a small-eyed pickerel has fewer calories than a wall-eyed pike. Simplify, instead of complicating, food preparation.

Tips for Cooking Up QTD Servings

❋ *In recipes, you may use small quantities of yogurt,* buttermilk, (instead of your daily quantity of 1 or 2 glasses of skim milk), lemon juice, grated rind of citrus fruits, vinegar, mustard, ketchup, chili sauce, horseradish, onion flakes, parsley flakes, pickle, pickle relish, dried herbs, seasonings. You may use thin slices of part-skim-milk mozzarella cheese for a cheeseburger, or as a melted topping for other dishes. Repeat: small quantities only, in QTD recipes It's best to use salt and any sodium seasonings sparingly.

❋ *In using skim milk or buttermilk* in recipes, such as drinks, and desserts, whatever amount you use in recipes that day should be subtracted from your total of 1 or 2 glasses per day—1 glass daily age 18 or over, 2 glasses per day under age 18.

❋ *In using cooking wine,* excellent for keeping certain foods such as meats, fish, and chicken moist for specific recipes, be sure that the food is cooked long enough so that the alcohol is cooked away (no longer any smell of alcohol left). This means that the alcohol calories will be cooked away, too (if aroma is not cooked away completely, the serving is not permitted on the Quick Teenage Diet because it would interfere with the most efficient working of the specific dynamic action of protein in this diet).

✻ *In seasoning foods,* take advantage of the many brands now available of "seasoned salt," "seasoned pepper," "lemon-pepper marinade," and other prepared seasonings in shaker bottles. Always use such seasonings lightly.

✻ *Simple broiling, roasting, baking, boiling* of meats, poultry, and fish are still the preferred ways for most overweights on the Quick Teenage Diet, so consider those ways of food preparation basic. The recipes here (and those created by you or whoever prepares your food) are merely to add variety for those who seek it.

✻ *In general, the longer you cook meat,* the fewer the calories. For example, "well done" steak and hamburger have fewer calories than when cooked "rare."

✻ *Some recipes with one kind of meat*—beef, for instance—may also be used with lean veal, lamb, even poultry and fish in some cases. Use your good judgment.

✻ *More complicated recipes* that take a lot of time in preparation or cooking are not included here. My recommendation is that you concentrate on losing pounds and inches, not on winning any cooking prizes. However, that's entirely your choice—if you have fun cooking up and creating your own more complicated QTD recipes, enjoy!

A Sampling of Quick Teenage Diet Recipes

MEATS

Hamburgers

Use lean meat from which fat has been trimmed before grinding. The meat can be ground beef, veal, or lamb. Season sparingly with salt, pepper, and any other seasonings of your choice. Make patties of no more than 4 ounces of meat. Broil, or pan-fry in a no-fat pan. (Don't ever use a roll or bread with the hamburger while on the Quick Teenage Diet, nor any bread crumbs or other non-protein filler. It's fine to mix in an egg, if desired, using a smaller quantity of meat than without the egg.)

Cottage-Cheese-Burger

Split a raw hamburger sideways. Spread bottom half of meat with about a ¼-in. layer of cottage cheese (add a little ketchup to cottage cheese, if desired). Cover with other half of hamburger. Pan-fry in no-fat pan. Turn over with a spatula when bottom of hamburger is well browned. Cover top (browned side) with another ¼-in. layer of cottage cheese (mixed with a little ketchup, if wanted). Place lid over pan. Serve when bottom is browned. Sprinkle a little paprika on cottage cheese top.

Mozzarella-Burger

Make the same way as Cottage-Cheese-Burger, but use thin, flat slices of mozzarella cheese (made of part skim milk) for middle and top layers instead of cottage cheese. Sprinkle a little powdered oregano or pizza spice on top of Mozzarella-Burger instead of paprika, if preferred.

Ketchup-Burger, and other variations

Mix a little ketchup (to taste) with the hamburger meat before cooking.

Chili-Burger: Instead of ketchup, you might prefer to

mix in a little mustard, or chili sauce, but never overload the hamburger with spices and seasonings.

Pickle-Burger: As another change, mince a sweet pickle (or piece of any pickle) with the lean hamburger meat before broiling or pan-frying in no-fat pan.

Herb-Burger: In addition to, or instead of the minced pickle, you can sprinkle in some onion flakes and/or parsley flakes with the meat, for a different flavor. You may sparingly mix any dried herbs you like with the lean chopped meat before cooking.

Wine-Burger: Mix a teaspoonful of red cooking wine and onion flakes, parsley flakes, or dried herbs with the lean hamburger meat, adding a little salt and pepper to taste. Pan-fry the meat until well browned, making sure that any alcoholic aroma has disappeared (meaning that the alcohol calories have cooked away). Makes a tasty, juicy hamburger with a tangy flavor change.

Top any of these hamburger recipe variations with a thin slice of mozzarella cheese and melt it, if you desire.

Frankfurters with Sauce

1 tablespoon ketchup
½ teaspoon mustard
¼ chopped dill pickle, or chopped sweet pickle

Mix ingredients into a sauce. Broil 1 or 2 frankfurters until almost done. Spread the thick sauce over frankfurters, and broil for 1 or 2 minutes until ready to serve sizzling hot.

Meat Loaf

½ lb. lean ground beef, lamb, or veal
2 tablespoons ketchup
1 teaspoon onion flakes
1 teaspoon parsley flakes
1 egg lightly beaten
Salt and pepper to taste

Combine ingredients in small no-stick baking dish. Bake in moderate oven (350°) until brown, about 20 minutes. Drain off any fat that may be in juice in dish. Makes 2 to 3 servings.

Aspic—Meat (or Chicken, Turkey, Fish, Seafood)

1 cup chicken bouillon	½ cup cooked cubed meat,
1 envelope unflavored gel-	chicken, turkey, fish, or
atin	seafood
¾ teaspoon vinegar	Salt, paprika, herbs to taste

Dissolve the gelatin in the broth. Add salt, paprika, herbs to taste. Chill in refrigerator. When gelatin is thickened but not firm, add cubes of lean meat (all visible fat removed), chicken or turkey (all skin removed), fish, or seafood (shrimp, crabmeat, or lobster). Or you may combine any leftovers of meat, chicken, and so on. Chill mixture until firmly set, and sprinkle a little paprika on top just before serving.

Meat-Cheese Rolls

Use very thin, cold slices of beef, lamb, or veal—and lay out flat like a pancake. Cover meat slices with a thin layer of cottage cheese seasoned with herbs and spices of your choice, such as chopped chives, paprika, rosemary, chili or curry powder. Roll up the slices of meat, refrigerate the rolls, and cut into bite-size pieces when ready to serve.

Meat-Egg-Rolls

Mince a hard-boiled egg with a little ketchup and/or mustard to moisten and make into a paste. Spread the egg mixture on a very thin slice of cold beef, veal, or lamb. Roll the meat slowly with the egg filling. Refrigerate the roll, and cut into bite-size pieces when ready to serve.

Veal Scallopini

In heated no-stick pan, place slice of veal scallopini (veal sliced thin) from which all fat has been trimmed. Add a teaspoon of white or red cooking wine. Simmer until all alcohol aroma has disappeared from the wine, and meat is tender. Salt to taste.

Meat Bake (Beef, Lamb, or Veal)

1 slice about ¼" thick of ¼ cup beef bouillon
  beef, lamb, or veal 1 teaspoon onion flakes
Salt, pepper, and paprika 1 teaspoon parsley flakes
  to taste ½ teaspoon lemon juice

Trim all fat off slice of meat. Season meat lightly with salt, pepper, and a little paprika. In a warmed no-stick pan, brown the meat over a high heat, turning a few times until browned.

Place the browned meat in a non-stick shallow baking pan. Combine and stir together the bouillon, lemon juice, onion flakes, and parsley flakes; pour the mixture over the meat. Cover the pan and place in moderate (330°) oven for 10 to 15 minutes, then serve.

Broiled Marinated Lamb

1 lamb steak (or lamb chop)
2 tablespoons wine vinegar
½ teaspoon bay leaf flakes
½ teaspoon onion flakes
½ teaspoon parsley flakes
Garlic powder
Rosemary
Thyme

Trim all visible fat off the meat, and place the lamb steak or chop in a shallow pan. Separately, combine the wine vinegar, bay leaf, onion and parsley flakes, with dashes of garlic powder, rosemary, and thyme. Spoon the mixture on the meat. Let the meat "marinate" in the sauce for a few hours in the refrigerator, with pan covered. Then broil until meat is cooked through, basting with the mixture in the pan once or twice while broiling. Serve, spooning any leftover mixture over the meat.

POULTRY

Broiled Chicken Legs and Thighs

4 chicken parts (legs and thighs)
Salt and pepper to taste
Oregano powder
Garlic powder
1 teaspoon lemon juice
1 teaspoon cooking wine

Place chicken parts in shallow non-stick pan, salt and pepper very lightly. Dust parts lightly with oregano powder (crushed oregano) and garlic powder. Broil on top rack for 10 minutes, basting every few minutes with the mixture of lemon juice and cooking wine. Turn chicken parts and broil on other side for another 10 minutes, continuing the basting. Place pan on lower rack, broil 10 minutes longer, then serve. Have one chicken part (moderate size) per meal, either reheating leftover parts or eating cold. Don't eat skin—preferably remove skin before cooking, but if not, remove before eating. Makes 4 servings.

Chicken Soy

Paint 4 moderate-size chicken parts (legs and thighs) with a soy sauce that doesn't contain sugar (check label of brand). Brown in broiler. When parts are browned, place in non-stick pan that contains a little water, and bake in moderate (350°) oven until tender. Makes 4 servings.

Herbed Chicken Livers

1 portion chicken livers	1 teaspoon parsley flakes
1 tablespoon herbed cooking wine	Salt and pepper to taste

Place chicken livers in shallow non-stick pan. Combine the herbed cooking wine and parsley flakes, and pour over the chicken livers. Place pan a few inches from flame, and broil for about 2 minutes on one side. Turn over livers with a spoon (not fork), baste with liquid in pan, and broil for about 2 more minutes until livers are cooked through. Serve, with a little salt and pepper if desired.

Chopped Chicken Livers

2 portions broiled chicken livers	1 tablespoon no-fat chicken broth
1 hard-boiled egg	Herbs and spices to taste

In a bowl combine the broiled chicken livers (slightly warm or cool), hard-boiled egg, and broth, sprinkling on herbs and spices to your taste. Chop to the fineness you like best, mixing ingredients lightly with a fork until all are well combined and hold together. Chill and serve. Serves 2.

Chicken-Deviled Eggs

1 hard-boiled egg
½ to 1 teaspoon ketchup (as needed)
Pinch of dry or regular light mustard

1 tbsp. finely chopped cooked chicken (or turkey)
Paprika

Cut hard-boiled egg in half lengthwise. Remove yolks. Mix yolks thoroughly with the ketchup, mustard, and chopped chicken, adding salt and paprika to taste. Place the mixture in the egg whites, mound to fill. Sprinkle on a little paprika for extra color.

Chicken-Egg Soup

1 cup no-fat chicken bouillon
⅓ cup water

1 heaping tablespoon diced cooked chicken
1 egg
Salt, pepper, and herbs to taste

Combine the chicken bouillon and water in a small pot, add the diced chicken, and heat to the boiling point. Then slowly add beaten egg, and stir the mixture over moderate flame for 2 to 3 minutes. Serve, adding salt, pepper, and herbs to taste.

Baked Herbed Fish

1 portion fish fillet or fish steak (your favorite type)	½ teaspoon parsley flakes
	Onion salt
	Lemon juice
1 teaspoon white cooking wine	Pepper or paprika

Combine the wine, parsley flakes, and onion salt (lightly, to taste) and anoint the fish on both sides with the liquid. Place fish in shallow non-stick baking pan, topping the fillet with any of the mixture left over. Bake in hot oven (375°–400°) for about 10 to 15 minutes, until fish is cooked through. Serve with a little fresh lemon juice squeezed on top, if desired—or sprinkle top with a little pepper or paprika.

Broiled Salmon (canned or fresh)

1 portion canned salmon, or leftover broiled fresh salmon	Onion salt
	Salt and pepper to taste
	1 tablespoon plain yogurt
Lemon juice	Paprika

Preheat broiler. Drain can of red salmon (or use leftover broiled fresh salmon) and spread portion in shallow non-stick pan, breaking up the salmon into flakes. Sprinkle on lemon juice, onion salt (or onion flakes), and a little salt and pepper to taste. Cover top with dots of plain yogurt sprinkled lightly with paprika. Place pan about 3 in. or more from burner, and broil slowly for 6 to 8 minutes until salmon is very hot. Serve with a little fresh lemon juice sprinkled on top, if desired.

Broiled Tuna

Follow the same (preceding) recipe as for salmon, using water-packed tuna instead.

Fish Chowder

1 cup clear clam broth (or chicken bouillon)
½ cup cubed chunks of leftover cooked fish
¼ cup skim milk
1 teaspoon onion flakes
1 teaspoon parsley flakes
Salt and pepper to taste

Combine all ingredients, stirring with a fork, in small pot. Heat over moderate flame to the boiling point, but don't boil. Serve, adding a little salt and pepper or other seasonings to your taste.

Shrimp Soup

6 medium cooked shrimps, cut into bite-size chunks
½ cup buttermilk
½ cup water
½ teaspoon powdered skim milk
1 small chopped sweet pickle
Dash of dry mustard, salt, parsley flakes
Paprika

Combine all ingredients in a small pot and heat slowly to the boiling point, but don't boil. Serve piping hot, topped with a little paprika for added color; add any seasoning desired, to taste.

To serve cold, let the cooked soup cool, then chill in refrigerator.

Dilled Salmon •

1 portion drained canned
   salmon (or leftover
   cooked salmon)
1 teaspoon dried dill

½ teaspoon lemon juice
Dash of vinegar
Salt and pepper to taste

Flake the salmon and combine with all ingredients
with a fork. Add salt and pepper, to taste.

Shrimps and Mozzarella

6 medium-size cooked
   shrimps
1 thin slice part-skim-milk
   mozzarella cheese

Paprika
Ketchup, chili or cocktail
   sauce

Place shrimps on broiler. Cut mozzarella into small
squares and place as "dots" on top of shrimps, then
sprinkle with a little paprika for color. Broil until mozzarella cheese is hot and bubbling, well melted. Serve,
with a little ketchup, chili sauce, or cocktail sauce, if
desired.

Clam Soup

1 cup clam juice or clam broth
1 heaping tablespoon minced clams (canned or fresh)
Celery salt

Place clam broth in small pot, stir in the minced clams,
and season to taste with celery salt (and any other herbs
or seasonings). Bring to boiling point over moderate

flame, but don't boil. Serve in bowl, topping with more celery salt or other seasonings to taste.

Scrambled Clams and Eggs

1 egg
1 tablespoon (or more) minced clams

1 tablespoon water or clam juice
Pepper and celery salt to taste

Combine raw egg, minced clams, liquid, and seasonings to your taste in a bowl, mixing loosely with a fork. Pour into heated non-stick pan, and heat over low flame until set, stirring with a wooden spatula if you prefer scrambled result. Serve hot, topping with a little celery salt or pepper if you wish.

Tarragon Baked Fish

1 fish fillet or steak (your favorite fish)
1 teaspoon lemon juice

½ teaspoon tarragon vinegar
Dried tarragon
Salt and pepper to taste

Place fish fillet or steak in non-stick shallow pan. Pour over the fish a mixture of the lemon juice, tarragon vinegar, and two pinches of dried tarragon. Sprinkle with salt and pepper to taste. Bake in hot oven (400°) for 8 to 10 minutes, occasionally basting with the liquid at bottom of pan, until fish is thoroughly cooked. Serve with a few drops of fresh lemon juice on top, adding a little more tarragon if desired.

Broiled Fillets

1 fish fillet or steak (your favorite fish)
⅛ cup chicken bouillon
1 teaspoon lemon juice

¼ teaspoon celery salt
¼ teaspoon paprika
Salt and pepper to taste

Place fillet in shallow non-stick pan, and pour over fish the pre-mixed liquid of the bouillon, lemon juice, and seasonings. Place pan about 3 inches under broiler, basting fish with the juice in the pan every couple of minutes until the fish is cooked through thoroughly (about 8 minutes). Salt and pepper to taste, and serve, pouring any remaining liquid in pan over the fish.

Baked Soy Fish

1 moderate-size fillet (your favorite fish)
1 teaspoon soy sauce (use brand that doesn't contain sugar; check label)

½ teaspoon fresh lemon juice
Celery salt
Paprika

Place fish in shallow non-stick pan. Combine mixture of about a teaspoon of soy sauce, the lemon juice, and a few dashes of celery salt and paprika. "Paint" the fish thoroughly with the soy mixture before cooking, and once or twice while in the oven. Place in hot oven (400°) for about 5 minutes, until fish is cooked through. If any sauce is left in pan, brush it over the fish, and serve hot.

Broiled Lobster Tails

1 lobster tail (thawed), large, or 2 small-size
1 tablespoon clam juice (or chicken bouillon, or ketchup)
½ teaspoon lemon juice
Dash of Worcestershire sauce
Dash of curry powder
¼ teaspoon lemon juice
Salt and pepper to taste

Split lobster tail shell lengthwise (to help prevent curling) and place in shallow pan. Combine all other ingredients, and pour mixture over lobster tail. Place pan about 3 inches from flame, and broil 6 to 8 minutes, basting meat with sauce about 3 times while broiling. Serve hot with a little fresh lemon juice sprinkled on top, and salt and pepper to taste.

Broiled Garlic Shrimps

6 medium-size raw peeled shrimps
½ cup no-fat chicken bouillon
½ teaspoon white cooking wine
Garlic salt
Lemon juice

Place shrimps in a shallow bowl. Mix all other ingredients, and pour mixture over shrimps. Place bowl in refrigerator an hour or more so shrimps can soak in the mixture. Then place shrimps in shallow no-stick baking pan, and pour remaining sauce over shrimps. With pan about 3 inches from flame, broil for about 6 to 8 minutes until shrimps are pink and cooked through, meanwhile basting several times with the remaining sauce. Serve with a few drops of fresh lemon juice, and sprinkle with more garlic salt if desired.

Baked Scallops

¼ lb. scallops
1 tablespoon beef bouillon
1 tablespoon white cooking wine

1 teaspoon onion flakes
½ teaspoon parsley flakes
Celery salt
Lemon juice

Place scallops in non-stick baking pan. Mix thoroughly all other ingredients, and pour mixture over the scallops. Cover pan, and place in moderate oven (350°) for 6 to 8 minutes, basting with the mixture once or twice while baking. Serve piping hot, or if you like the scallops browned, place pan about 2 inches from broiler flame for 1 or 2 minutes. Place scallops on plate, pour on any remaining mixture, and add a few drops of fresh lemon juice if desired.

EGGS

Creamy Scrambled Eggs

1 egg
1 tablespoon skim milk or buttermilk
Salt and herbs to taste

Mix egg, milk and seasonings lightly. Pour into heated non-stick pan. Cook over moderate flame until tender, stirring occasionally with wooden spatula. Serve, and add salt and herbs to taste.

Deviled Eggs

2 hard-boiled eggs
¼ teaspoon light mustard*
¼ teaspoon vinegar

Salt to taste .
Paprika

Cut the hard-boiled eggs in half lengthwise. Scoop out the yolks and place in small bowl. Soften yolks with a fork, gradually adding the mustard and vinegar, and a few dashes of paprika and salt, if desired. Place the softened mixture back in the egg whites, mounding up and sprinkling tops with paprika for added color. Chill and serve, adding any other seasonings desired.

* Instead of mustard, you might prefer to use ½ teaspoon of ketchup or chili sauce.

Egg-Lemon Soup

1 cup chicken consommé
1 egg
½ teaspoon lemon juice

Salt, pepper, and herbs to taste

Heat the broth to the boiling point. Beat together the egg and lemon juice, and pour into consommé. Stir mixture constantly over heat until slightly thickened. Serve piping hot, adding salt, pepper, and herbs to taste.

Jelly Omelet

2 eggs
1 tablespoon skim milk or buttermilk (optional)
Salt

1 tablespoon artificially sweetened jam or jelly (any flavor)
Artificial granulated sugar or cinnamon

Beat the eggs until light, adding a tablespoon of skim milk or buttermilk if desired for extra fluffiness. Add a little salt. Pour into heated non-stick pan. As eggs cook over moderate flame, keep lifting the edges with a wooden spatula, letting the liquid run under. Shake pan

204

occasionally to keep bottom of eggs from sticking. When eggs are almost cooked, but still a little soft on top, spoon the jam or jelly onto one side, and with spatula fold the other side over the jelly filling. If you prefer eggs browned, place pan under broiler for 30 seconds or less, removing as soon as top is slightly browned. Serve, and sprinkle with granulated artificial sweetener or cinnamon.

Eggs with Mozzarella Cheese

2 eggs	1 thin slice part-skim-milk
1 tablespoon skim milk	mozzarella cheese, cut in
	small pieces
	Paprika or oregano

In a bowl, loosely mix the eggs, skim milk, and small pieces of mozzarella cheese until well combined. Pour into heated non-stick pan, and cook over moderate flame, stirring mixture occasionally with a wooden spatula—until eggs are set to your liking. Serve topped with a sprinkle of paprika or oregano.

Cold Eggs and Fish

2 hard-boiled eggs	Celery salt, pepper, chili
½ cup of well-drained	powder
salmon, water-packed	Fresh lemon juice
tuna, or water-drained	
sardines	

Cut hard-boiled eggs in half lengthwise. Place yolks in a bowl, and add the salmon or other fish of your choice, along with a little celery salt, pepper, and dash of chili powder. Mash all together well with a fork. Stuff mixture into the hard-cooked egg whites. Serve topped with a sprinkling of chili powder, and a few drops of fresh-squeezed lemon juice. (Instead of chili powder, you may use paprika, curry powder, or any seasoning of your choice.) Makes 2 servings.

Bologna and Scrambled Eggs (and other variations)

1 large, thin slice of bolo-gna (or 2 small slices)	1 teaspoon water
1 egg	Salt to taste

In non-stick pan, cook bologna slowly until much of the fat is drained out. Pat the bologna with paper towel to wipe off remaining fat, then cut into small pieces. Mix together the egg, water, bits of bologna, and a little salt if desired. Pour mixture into dry, heated non-stick pan, and stir occasionally with wooden spatula over moderate flame until as firm as you like. (Instead of water, you may use a teaspoon of ketchup if you wish.)

Instead of bologna, use ½ frankfurter, chipped beef, or other meat, or leftover diced chicken or turkey.

Well-drained salmon, tuna, or sardines may be added to the scrambled eggs instead of bologna, as desired.

Bouillon plus Egg

1 cup chicken or beef bouillon
1 hard-boiled egg
Seasonings to taste

Heat bouillon to the boiling point, then add a sliced hard-boiled egg, and seasonings to your taste; simmer for 1 or 2 minutes to heat the egg, then serve.

COTTAGE CHEESE

Cottage Cheese Mixtures

Creamed or "diet" cottage cheese is a versatile protein food that is delicious with any number of seasonings and other protein foods added. Here are a few suggestions to start you creating some of your own favorite mixtures for practically any meal or snack. It's a good idea to make more of the mix than one serving and to keep the remainder in the refrigerator as a snack when wanted.

Add cinnamon and granulated artificial sweetener to taste.

"Herbed Cottage Cheese" can be made with any number of herbs and seasonings. The cottage cheese can be mixed with minced chives, paprika, rosemary, thyme, onion flakes, parsley flakes, chili powder, and so on and on for an infinite variety of seasoned cottage cheese. If you wish, you can also add ketchup, chili sauce, or a little dry mustard in small quantities.

Mix with artificially sweetened jam or jelly.

Mix with artificially sweetened flavoring, whatever fruit or other flavorings available that you prefer.

Add to artificially sweetened gelatin dessert when the gelatin is at the point of being slightly thickened; beat with a rotary beater until thoroughly mixed in, then chill until set. (*Yogurt* may be used in this recipe instead of cottage cheese for a change if desired.)

Mix with minced clams, seasoned to your taste.

Mix with diced chicken, bits of bologna, any diced meat, leftover fish, drained salmon, tuna, sardines, or shellfish . . . with practically any of the foods in the QTD listing.

Chilled Cottage Cheese Loaf

1 lb creamed cottage
  cheese
1 egg
½ teaspoon powdered
  cinnamon

Liquid or granulated artificial sweetening (equivalent of 2 teaspoons of
  sugar)
Vanilla flavoring
Salt

In a blender (or using hand beater), combine the
cottage cheese, raw egg, cinnamon, artificial sweetener,
2 dashes of vanilla flavoring, and a dash of salt. Beat
until blended smooth, place in a bowl or loaf dish, and
keep in freezer. Ready to eat after an hour or more. In
moderate portions, about 4 servings.

Cottage Cheese Dip

1 cup cottage cheese
1 teaspoon lemon juice

1 packet (for 1 cup) of
  powdered beef broth or
  bouillon
Seasonings

Combine the ingredients with the creamed cottage
cheese, mixing well, adding a little water if needed for
a looser paste. Add seasonings to taste (onion flakes,
parsley flakes, garlic powder, rosemary, thyme, paprika—
or whatever herbs and seasonings you like best). Use as
a dip for cold shrimps or other seafood, as a sauce for
cubed chicken, meats, fish, as you wish.

Cottage Cheese Soup

1 cup chicken bouillon
¼ cup cottage cheese
Paprika, celery salt or other seasoning to taste

Heat the bouillon to the boiling point, turn down flame a little, and gradually stir in the cottage cheese. Keep stirring until the cheese is thoroughly blended with the liquid. Serve hot with a sprinkle of paprika, celery salt, or other seasoning on top. (Same recipe can be made with beef bouillon.)

DESSERTS

Coffee Fluff

1 cup black coffee (regular or no-caffeine)
1 egg
2 tablespoons non-fat dry milk
Cinnamon

Nutmeg (optional)
Artificial sweetener to taste (equal to about a tablespoon of sugar), in granulated or liquid form

Chill the coffee and pour into electric blender bowl. Add the raw egg and all other ingredients, including a dash of cinnamon. Run blender at medium speed for 2 to 3 minutes until mixture is thick and fluffy. Serve with a little more cinnamon or nutmeg on top.

Gelatin Dessert Ices

1 pkg. artificially sweetened gelatin dessert, any flavor
1 cup cold water

1 cup boiling water
½ teaspoon grated lemon peel
½ teaspoon lemon juice

Soften the gelatin in the boiling water, and stir steadily until gelatin is entirely dissolved. Stir in thoroughly the cold water, along with the lemon juice and grated lemon peel.

Place bowl in refrigerator until mixture is slightly thickened. Now beat the thickened mixture at moderate speed with an electric mixer until foamy (2 to 3 minutes, usually). Pour the fluffy mixture at once into individual serving dishes (makes 6 average-size servings), and set into the *freezer* compartment of the refrigerator. Servings are solid and ready to eat after 3 or more hours in freezer compartment.

QTD Ice Cream Stand-In

1 teaspoon unflavored gelatin	Salt
	½ cup non-fat dry milk
2 teaspoons cold skim milk	¼ cup water
½ cup skim milk	1 teaspoon lemon juice
2 tablespoons artificially sweetened flavoring, any flavor	Salt

In electric mixer bowl, combine the gelatin with the 2 teaspoons of cold skim milk, and soften with a fork. Heat the ½ cup of skim milk almost to the boiling point (but not to a boil), add the flavoring and a pinch of salt, then combine with the gelatin mixture. Chill in the refrigerator until slightly thickened. While chilling, combine the ½ cup of non-fat dry milk with the water and lemon juice; then whip in the electric mixer until stiff, which usually will take 5 minutes or more. Now fold the two mixtures together thoroughly. Spread the combination in refrigerator trays, and leave until frozen firm. Enjoy small servings.

Coffee Gelatin Dessert

1 envelope unflavored gelatin

2 tablespoons instant coffee (regular or non-caffeine)

⅛ teaspoon salt

1¾ cups water

Artificial sweetener, granulated or liquid, equal to ⅓ cup sugar

In a saucepan, mix together the gelatin, instant coffee, and salt. Add ½ cup of the water, and place over low heat, stirring until gelatin mixture is dissolved. Remove from heat (leave in saucepan), and stir in the remaining 1¼ cups of water, and the artificial sweetener. When thoroughly mixed, pour into 4 dessert dishes or a 2-cup mold or bowl. Chill until firm. Enjoy servings with meals, or between meals when wanted. Makes 4 servings.

Dessert Topping

¼ cup non-fat dry milk

¼ cup ice water

2 teaspoons granulated artificial sweetener (less or more to taste)

Combine the ingredients in bowl of an electric mixer, and beat at high speed until mixture is like whipped cream. Serve small amount on artificially sweetened gelatin dessert or other permitted QTD desserts.

QTD Frozen Custard

1½ teaspoons unflavored gelatin

2 tablespoons cold water

1 cup skim milk

1 egg, beaten

½ teaspoon granulated artificial sweetener (more or less, to your taste)

½ teaspoon vanilla flavoring

In a saucepan, mix the gelatin and cold water thoroughly. Heat the skim milk to the boiling point (but don't boil), then mix with the gelatin, a smoothly beaten egg, and the artificial sweetener. Over a very slow flame, keep stirring the mixture until it thickens, then stir in the vanilla flavoring. Pour the mixture into freezer ice tray. Stir every half-hour or so until the mixture is quite "solid," and ready to eat like frozen custard. Enjoy small portions.

DRINKS AND REFRESHERS

Flavored Milk

To a cup of ice-cold skim milk, add a teaspoonful (more or less, to taste) of artificially sweetened syrup, in your favorite flavor. Stir thoroughly. Add ice cubes if desired.

To a cup of ice-cold skim milk, add a teaspoonful of instant coffee (regular or non-caffeine). Mix thoroughly, adding ice cubes if desired.

Electric Blender Coolers

To a glass of artificially sweetened carbonated beverage in your favorite flavor, add ¼ cup of skim milk (or 1 teaspoon of non-fat dry milk), and 2 ice cubes. Mix in blender at high speed until thoroughly blended.

For a coffee cooler, combine ½ cup cold water, ½ cup skim milk, 1 teaspoon instant coffee (regular or non-caffeine), and 1 teaspoon of granulated artificial sweetener (or liquid to taste), with 2 ice cubes. Mix at high speed until thoroughly blended.

Soda Blends

In addition to enjoying artificially sweetened sodas in various flavors as they pour from the bottle, you can make your own combinations. For example, combine ½ glass of cola soda with ½ glass lemon soda . . . or ½ glass raspberry soda with ½ glass ginger ale . . . or ⅓ glass black cherry soda, ⅓ glass cola soda, and ⅓ glass lemon soda—with a thin slice of fresh lemon floating on top. Make up your own combinations as you wish.

QTD Thick Shake

¼ cup non-fat dry milk
1 tablespoon (more or less, to taste) of artificially sweetened syrup, any flavor

1 glass water
2 or 3 ice cubes

Combine all ingredients in electric blender, and mix for about 1 minute at high speed.

For a coffee-flavored thick shake, instead of the syrup, use a teaspoon of instant coffee (regular or no-caffeine), and artificial sweetener (granulated or liquid) to taste.

QTD Eggnog

1 cup skim milk
1 egg, white and yolk separated
1 teaspoon granulated artificial sweetener

⅛ teaspoon vanilla flavoring
1 ice cube
Nutmeg and cinnamon

In electric blender bowl, combine skim milk, beaten egg yolk, artificial sweetener, vanilla, and an ice cube. Beat until thoroughly blended and a litte thick. Beat the egg white separately until slightly stiff, then slowly fold the egg white into the mixture. Serve with a little nutmeg and cinnamon sprinkled on top.

Flavored Ice Cubes

Combine 2 or more glasses of artificially sweetened sodas in 2 (or more) flavor combinations such as grape soda and ginger ale. Pour into a freezer tray with an ice-cube divider. Freeze until solid; then enjoy 1 or more of the flavored ice cubes whenever you want a refresher.

As another variation, you can freeze artificially sweetened soda of any flavor in the ice-cube tray. Then enjoy the cubes as they are, or drop a few lemon soda ice cubes into a glass of cola soda—or any such combinations you care to dream up.

~~~~~~~~~~~~~~~~

As noted earlier, these recipes are just a starting point for you—to spur you to try your own *Quick Teenage Diet* creative cooking—if you're so inclined. Most of your foods will simply be broiled, baked, roasted, pan-fried without any fat, or boiled—according to the usual procedures. They all must be on the QTD foods listing, and must be prepared *absolutely* without butter, margarine, oils, gravies, rich sauces, or fats of any kind.

Of course, you can combine several QTD foods on one plate, or for one meal, as long as you keep portions small. For example, your dinner plate might contain 3 shrimps with cocktail sauce, a small hamburger, and a small portion of herbed cottage cheese.

Use the recipes as you enjoy them, and as they help you most. As always, the choice in QTD eating is *yours*. You might nickname your kitchen, after a diner specializing in diet recipes, "The Tiny Diney."

214

13

Talking It Over With the Doctor: Most-Asked Questions and the Answers

Over the years I have talked with many thousands of overweight teenagers in my office, in schools, in group discussions, in camps. In recent years I have given up active medical practice, in order to help the greatest possible number of overweights through writing, speaking, and consultation.

In talking with teenagers, I have found that certain questions seem to come up over and over again. Here are some of those asked most often which may occur to you, and the answers.

> *"I hate looking fat, Doctor, but at least it's not bad for my health . . . right?"*

Wrong! Excess fat and flab are bad for you, likely to bring on health problems not only in teen years but for the rest of a probably shortened life filled with greater physical suffering. New findings point to such tragic effects increasingly. A noted scientist reports, for instance, "Data from animal experiments indicate that the number of fat cells (adipocytes) may be programmed early in life and that an increase in the number of such cells will render the animal permanently obese (extremely fat) and make it exceedingly difficult to sustain weight reduction in later life."

A past president of the American Medical Association stated, "Cancer is the most dreaded disease in the United

States. But the greatest danger to the health is obesity." Aside from shortening life, bulging the belly, and spoiling looks and gracefulness, overweight tends to bring on serious sickness.

Concerned about personal suffering? It's even more important to get rid of excess fat and flab for health than for appearance's sake. Overweight increases body malformation, as it strains the muscles, bones, organs, and entire body structure. Foot, leg, and back pains and breakdowns are more likely among the overweights.

What happens inside your body may be even worse. Fat deposits all over your structure, from head and neck right down to legs and feet, make increased demands on blood pumped from the heart. Fat layers choke the heart and crowd the lungs, reducing ease of breathing, bringing on shortness of breath and puffing. The stomach swells up to as much as three times or more its normal size, pushing against the chest.

You're fortunate to be young, in your teens. You can help prevent the horrors of lasting overweight from happening to you. By slimming down now, and keeping slim, you may head off many physical, mental, and emotional ills. "Clogged with yesterday's excess," a warning goes, "the body drags the mind down with it."

"People tell me that, as a growing teenager, I should eat a lot. I'm afraid to diet and I'm getting fatter all the time. What can I do?"

Forget the false, old-fashioned idea that you must "Eat! Eat! Eat!" You *don't* need rich foods, big breakfasts, heavy full-course meals, in order to grow properly. Reject the bad advice of the ignorant and uninformed who think that "fat is good for you." Ignore the urgings of those who profit by selling high-calorie foods.

Unfortunately, you and your family are bombarded by advertising that pushes high-calorie foods at you, makes them seem wholesome, nutritious, and good for you. Don't believe it! Rich cakes, sugary drinks, buttery, greasy, predominantly high-calorie meals and snacks can sicken you as they build up unhealthy flab.

The public-minded Federal Communications Commissioner, Nicholas Johnson, has warned, "There's been a lot of talk recently about malnutrition in America. Yet people could let their television sets run for twenty-four hours a day and never discover that diets of starch and soda pop can be fatal." Resist the ads that would stuff you with fats. Follow the lead of a bright young man who said, "I have two eyes and a mind, which is one more eye and one more mind than television has." Think for yourself, and you'll "think thin" and eat to slim, not to fatten and sicken your body.

"Isn't it bad for me to lose weight quickly?"

Consider for yourself how ridiculous that fake fear is, and you'll realize that the quicker you get rid of excess weight, the better it is for you in every way. Picture yourself walking home from the supermarket, carrying 35 pounds of groceries. As you puff and pant because of the overloaded bags, you meet a friend and wail, "I've got to drop this 35 pounds of weight fast or my back will break." He says, "Oh, no, it's *bad* for you to put down that 35 pounds quickly. Put down a pound, then walk a block, then put down another pound, then . . ." By the time you put down that 35 pounds, one pound at a time, your back would feel "broken," you'd be aching all over —or collapsed completely on the sidewalk.

Realize that not only does your body have to "carry" extra fat (whether it's 35 lb., 20, 10, or whatever), but also that each fat cell has a capillary vessel carrying blood to it. Extra fat means extra blood flowing through your arteries and veins, and an extra strain on the heart, as the additional blood must be pumped through the system. The quicker you take off those excess pounds of fat, and get rid of your extra fat cells, the quicker your blood pressure will go down.

"I'm afraid of losing weight, then gaining again. Isn't it unhealthy and dangerous to go up and down in weight?"

The unhealthy and dangerous part is being over-weight. See-sawing in total weight won't hurt you as long as you reach ideal weight and stay slim eventually. Say your ideal weight is 110 lb. and you weigh 140 lb. If you reduce to 110 lb., then gain to 140 lb. again over a 6-month period, you're still better off than at the start, because your average weight during the 6 months was 125 lb. instead of 140—and for that time, your body and organs were relieved from supporting that 15 lb. of excess fat.

What usually happens, though, is that you'd go down from 140 lb. to 110 lb., then maybe back up to 120 lb. if you let go. But then you'd probably go down again until you settled at 110–115 lb.

The fact is that any alert doctor who examines you for the first time, and finds you overweight, will probably tell you to reduce—without asking how many times you've lost and gained before. So don't worry about "up-and-down" hurting you—concentrate on getting *down* to ideal weight on the Quick Teenage Diet.

"Won't my skin sag if I lose a lot of weight?"

As a teenager, you're lucky, because your skin is more elastic and resilient. There's very little chance that losing weight will cause your skin to "sag" or "hang" or "loosen." The big danger is that you will pile on increasing pounds of fat as you grow older. Then, if you reduce at a later age (whether you lose weight quickly or slowly), faint stretch marks may remain in the skin. That's another good reason to get rid of excess fat and bulging inches *now*.

"Won't I feel weak and headachy from reducing?"

Many imagined ills appear when people deprive themselves of anything, whether it be rich, fattening foods or other treats. A fat teenager told me, "I developed a 'hunger headache' from not eating, so I had to eat a big fudge sundae to chase the headache." I pointed out that her headache was imagined, just an excuse to eat the ice cream—because if it had really been a "hunger headache," she could have chased it just as well with a hard-boiled egg, some cottage cheese, or other foods listed on the Quick Teenage Diet. She laughed as she realized the truth of this, went back on her diet, and slimmed down beautifully—never complained of a "hunger headache" again.

A heavy young man told me, "I looked at my tongue in the mirror and it looked peculiar. I figured something was wrong, so I broke my diet." I examined his tongue, and nothing was wrong. I asked, "Did you ever look at your tongue when you were fat?" "No," he admitted. "It looked just as 'peculiar' then," I assured him, "so stop worrying about 'symptoms' that don't exist." He went back on his diet and continued losing weight.

If you're overweight and feel "weak," it's probably from carrying that terrific burden of excess fat. If you think you feel weak from dieting, have a snack of one of the permitted foods, not cookies or cake or a fat sandwich. If you really feel weak or dizzy, 2 ounces of orange juice or a hard candy should pick you up quickly. If weakness or any other symptom persists, see your doctor immediately, as you may be ill—but not likely from dieting.

"Am I right in fearing to diet because it may put too much stress and strain on me?"

If you have no special physical or mental health disorders, there's undoubtedly far more strain in being fat, because your worries about it create a kind of stress that affects your metabolism negatively. This simple scientific explanation may interest you:

Such overweight stress, affecting the metabolism, increases the production of extra hormones. This in turn spurs the adrenals to produce more adrenalin, raising the blood sugar. To cope with the blood sugar, the pancreas pours out extra insulin. This insulin turns some of the sugar into energy but converts the rest to fat.

One of the first signs of overweight is hyperglycemia, involving excess sugar and a strain on the pancreas—which may lead to early diabetes. Under special medical testing, many obese individuals tend to have "a high glucose tolerance test," often indicating eventual diabetes.

The high production of fat surrounds the muscle cells and tissues and makes it difficult for the sugar to enter the muscle. This also means more sugar in the blood. The high sugar again is transformed into fats that are deposited in the body.

Some scientists state that people are definitely not "born to be fat," that overeating (hyperphagia) produces the large fat cells, and a great unhealthy number of them. So you'd better worry about this kind of burdensome body stress, rather than the "strain" of restricting your overeating.

"I'm forty pounds overweight; how much weight is it safe for me to take off?"

You should start immediately to take off *all* your excess pounds. You may wish to do this in stages, as noted earlier. It's *unsafe* to stay fat. Take it all off—now. Here's a typical case of what happened when a teenage boy lost 75 lb.

I am writing this letter to tell you how much your diet helped my boyfriend. George and I are both high school seniors. He is 6′ 1″ and his weight was 245 lb. He went on your diet and now he weighs 170—a loss of 75 lb.! This is the first time he hasn't been overweight in his whole life, and we wanted to express our thanks.

"Some family problems came up, so I ate to forget my troubles."

Being fat and overeating add to your troubles. Stuffing yourself with high-calorie foods won't chase them away. One of the best ways to handle your troubles is to get rid of your overweight problems, since you'll be able to tackle life better when you're healthier, more energetic. Get interested in other pursuits—walking, sports, writing, hobbies, school committees, whatever appeals most to you. Feeding your face is a poor excuse and the worst way to handle troubles effectively.

"How come my skinny friend eats as much as she wants of anything she wants—and never gets fat?"

In the first place, it's wasteful to spend a single second envying someone else. Your overweight problem is your own, and only you can correct it. In the second place, I questioned the "skinny friend" who was with my overweight patient. The slim girl said, "Yes, I eat anything I want"—but when I asked in detail about her eating habits, I found that she really didn't "want" much. When I totaled up her average day of eating, it was still under 1,000 calories.

You must concentrate on changing your own eating habits. Don't worry about anyone else's eating patterns, since each individual is different. There is a world of difference between living to eat and eating to live—and you must learn how to eat to live *slim*. The Quick Teenage Diet, after a week or two, will change the eating patterns that made you fat in the past.

> "How can I stick to a diet when the school lunchroom doesn't serve the foods I need to eat?"

It's true that most school lunchrooms offer foods that put on weight—such as macaroni and cheese, chicken croquettes, mashed potatoes, and heavy gravy. Nutritionists should know better, but they either have the old-fashioned notion that youngsters should be stuffed with fats, or, more likely, are not able to do anything to improve high-calorie menus.

You know what you should be eating (certainly after reading this book), and can easily handle the problem yourself. In the lunchroom, you can probably find some foods permitted on QTD—hamburger without gravy or roll, cottage cheese, frankfurter without roll, and more. But, aside from that, you can bring food from home—hard-boiled eggs, cottage cheese, a chicken leg, cold sliced meat—no problem at all. Some foods can be carried in a small Thermos. The reward of slimness is worth far more than any amount of inconvenience.

> "Won't using 'The Pill' make me fatter?"

Along with other effects in the body, "The Pill" tends to increase water retention, but never adds fat or muscle.

You can counteract any weight-increase effects due to water retention by eating a little less than your ideal weight calorie total and cutting down on salt and sodium products. Eliminate ketchup, mustard, M.S.G., salty foods in general, and use very little salt on your food. Drink a lot of water to keep washing out wastes. With these steps, it's not likely that you can rightfully blame "The Pill" for putting on weight.

"What can I do about putting on weight during my menstrual period?"

Teenage girls usually ask me this question, to which the answers are clear and comforting. Some girls put on 3 to 5 pounds just before the menses, and it's especially disturbing if one is dieting. Please don't be upset if this is the case with you (it doesn't happen with everybody). First, realize that this is very temporary, occurs just for a few days a month.

Second, you can counteract the weight increase by avoiding all foods with a high percentage of sodium or salt—ketchup, mustard, salt itself, cocktail sauces, relishes, M.S.G., anything containing sodium. That precaution will diminish a water-retaining effect that adds pounds on the scale.

Third, stay rigidly on the Quick Teenage Diet, and you'll lose more water than with any other way of dieting. The high-protein eating acts as a natural diuretic, increasing water discharge. If you are still concerned, see your physician, who may prescribe a mild diuretic drug.

Above all, don't be discouraged that you are gaining weight; never forget that such gain is temporary, for a few days only. When the menstruation period ends, you may have a sudden drop in weight of 3 to 10 pounds if you haven't indulged but have stayed rigidly with QTD eating.

*"Is it okay to nap a lot when dieting, since when
I'm sleeping I'm not eating?"*

No, don't sleep more than 8 hours in every 24, since
when you're sleeping you're not using up many calories.
You're much better off taking a brisk walk instead of a
nap, preferably with a friend for pleasant company.
Walking energetically, you'll use up more calories. Getting enough sleep (average of 8 hours a night) is good
for everybody, but getting too much sleep can actually
be *unhealthy,* aside from not using up enough calories.

A noted scientific study reported that "a person who
sleeps 10 or more hours a night may be snoozing his
way into a heart attack or stroke." The figures showed
that people who slept 10 or more hours a night were up
to four times as likely to suffer a heart attack or stroke as
those who slept 7 hours a night—particularly if they were
overweight.

*"Does overweight affect sexual desire and ca-
pacity?"*

There are so many factors that affect sexual capacity
that no one facet such as overweight can be named as
the cause of sexual inadequacy. While overweight cannot
be blamed completely, there's no question that being fat
may have a devastating sexual effect on boys and girls.
Overweight boys tend to be shy and uncertain of their
sexual ability.

Girls have two basic problems regarding sex when
overweight. First, they are often ashamed of their appearance and seldom go out with boys, often pretending they
don't want to date. They usually avoid bathing suits, and
are depressed about the way they look. Secondly, the
overweight young woman, feeling unattractive, may say
that she's not interested in the opposite sex, or feels that

she is sexually inadequate even though that really may not be true.

The situation changes in 99 percent of cases when the boy or girl slims down, and enjoys not only better looks, a more attractive figure, but a surge of vigor, vitality, and interest. Instead of worrying about the sexual aspects, the first step is to trim down to ideal weight and better health. As a lovely, newly slim teenage patient told me, "I finally decided that I wanted to have 'real boyfriends' instead of 'just good friends'! It worked out that way for me."

"Should a mentally disturbed overweight teenager diet?"

With mental illness, as with physical illness, I advise repeatedly that the teenager should be under the care of the personal physician, who will provide dieting advice and other care according to the individual case. Some mentally disturbed teenagers are fat, but others hate to eat and are excessively thin (this involves a fear and phobia about food, called "anorexia nervosa").

When a fat youngster tells me, "I have to eat because I'm nervous," I know that usually he's only fooling himself. Such overweights generally have few outside interests or activities. They concentrate too much on eating. They should reduce quickly, and that invariably chases the so-called "nervousness." They may slip back after losing some weight, but by trying again they eventually achieve permanent success.

If your doctor checks you out as healthy, mentally and physically, I urge you to put aside a weak excuse such as that "dieting makes me nervous." Just one week on the Quick Teenage Diet, with the exhilarating loss of 5 or more pounds, will drive away your "nervousness."

"Is it worth it going to a teenage slimming camp?"

I recommend a good slimming camp for many over-weight teenagers, girls and boys. A helpful fact is that all the campers are fat to start with, to a greater or lesser extent. Shame of body exposure because of bulkiness tends to vanish. All the overweights start from scratch and vie with each other in weight loss. There is no teasing or taunting. Together they work to increase their capacity for exercise, and engage in more strenuous, more sustained activity—as much as 80 percent of each day.

In a controlled camp situation, meals are low in calories, and there are no tempting high-calorie treats around. It becomes difficult, if not impossible, to go on an eating binge. Thus, eating habits tend to become fixed at low intake. In the camps I have checked, weight losses ranged from 14 to 55 pounds in 8 weeks.

Unfortunately, when they come home, the same temptations exist that made the campers fat in the past. At this point, particularly, I urge that the overweight girl or boy go immediately on the Quick Teenage Diet. This continues the pattern of losing weight rapidly and avoiding self-indulgence in rich foods. Then, after switching to Keep-Slim Eating, the Quick Teenage Diet is always available if weight creeps up at any time.

"How can I possibly keep dieting when I'm a guest at meals in a friend's house?"

The answer can be boiled down to three words: "No, thank you." There's nothing wrong with saying no politely when you are offered food prohibited on your diet. If you "just can't refuse," then make a pretense of eating, taking a very small helping, and leaving most of the food on the plate (it won't hurt you at all to skip a meal).

Even a leading etiquette authority says about dining out, "Eat what you wish and how much you wish"—and no more.

"Shouldn't I fear getting 'iron deficiency anemia' from dieting?"

Some advertisers promoting fake fears for their own profit warn about dangers of "iron deficiency anemia," especially among teens. This is self-serving nonsense as applied to the average teenager. If you are deficient in iron, your doctor's checkup would have shown it. Dieting doesn't adversely affect the hemoglobin or iron content of the blood among normal teens who have no bleeding troubles.

Actually, the average overweight teenager has too much blood in quantity, and often of undesirable quality, a condition called polycythemia, or too many blood cells. Concentrate on getting slim, without worries about fake fears (again, if you're not feeling well, your doctor will treat you). Carlyle said, "I grow daily to honor facts more and more, and theory less and less." My dieting recommendations are based on the *facts* of slimming success, not on hazy theory or advertising scares.

"How can I resist tempting but fattening foods?"

A magazine cartoon showed an angry fat wife saying to her frowning, thin husband, "That *'yellow scum'* on top of your asparagus happens to be hollandaise sauce!" It proves that different people regard food in different ways—what is one person's gourmet dish is another's "scum." More and more people regard the look and taste of rich, calorie-heavy foods as undesirable.

Try to change your own viewpoint. For instance, on

Keep-Slim Eating, you can look at that goo on asparagus as tempting hollandaise sauce—or as "yellow scum" that adds *hundreds* of calories and spoils the sweet, natural flavor of only 20 calories of delicious, fresh-tasting asparagus. Ask yourself, is it really worth staying heavy for the sake of swallowing high-calorie sauces and other rich, fattening foods?

"I joined a famous dieting club and followed the diet given to me. How is it that I GAINED weight during the month I was on it?"

The diet given to you added up to about 1,300 calories daily—and since my Keep-Slim calculations allot you only 1,100 calories a day to maintain ideal weight for your height and age, of course you gained weight. I have heard from hundreds of members of this dieting club who didn't lose weight—even gained on the diet. In the first place, if they lost a pound or two the first week, and nothing thereafter, even gaining a pound or two, they became disgusted and went back to overeating.

In the second place, they were alloted too many calories for effective slimming. Other so-called "reducing diets" I have checked allow 2,400–2,700 calories for teenagers 5' to 5' 6" in height, over twice as many calories as required for effective slimming. Somehow many nutritionists, and some individuals in the medical profession, still don't seem to realize that the body doesn't burn up as much food as they believe—so they overfeed overweights on their "reducing diets"—which specify too many calories.

When you follow the Quick Teenage Diet correctly, you lose pounds and inches quickly, since you are eating many fewer calories. Also, you are burning up calories faster because of the specific dynamic action of protein.

"Why is it that every time I have a fight with my parents or someone else, I go on an eating binge?"

If you think about it, you'll probably realize that you feel that you are punishing your parents (or friends) by stuffing food into yourself. Actually you are punishing yourself, aren't you? The best solution is to slim down quickly. When you stop being angry at yourself for overeating and being fat, you're less likely to be angry at others—or to punish yourself by overeating when you're upset about anything

"I lost 10 pounds my first week on the Quick Teenage Diet, then went a week without losing weight, although I dieted carefully—then suddenly I lost 12 pounds in 3 days! What made that happen?"

This happens once in a while with dieters who tend to retain water before a sudden, huge weight drop. As you dieted correctly, fat was being burned in your body, and the oxidation was producing water which was being retained in your body, as occurs with a small percentage of dieters. Then suddenly your system released the retained fat and water, resulting in a 12-pound weight loss in 3 days. Staying on QTD reducing, you should now lose weight rapidly and steadily rather than in one sudden drop.

This emphasizes the importance of staying with the Quick Teenage Diet even if you reach a plateau in weight loss. If you are following the diet instructions precisely, you will lose pounds—in your case a total of 22 pounds in 2 weeks, even though you were concerned during the second week that the numbers weren't going down on the scale.

"I've lost 14 pounds already on the Quick Teen-age Diet, but haven't had a daily bowel movement. Is this all right?"

You're doing great! Just realize as a matter of common sense that with the SDA of protein on this quick-reducing diet, fat is being burned up more swiftly and is being flushed out with a greater flow of liquids. Thus there is probably less residue. If, as happens occasionally, you don't have a bowel movement for a few days, don't start worrying about it. If it's your habit to have a daily bowel movement, nature will make adjustments and you'll probably soon resume having a daily movement. It's nothing to be concerned about.

If you are bothered about not having the daily movement, take milk of magnesia as specified on the package label. Don't take harsh laxatives—that's neither desirable nor necessary.

"I've read that 'obesity is a disease and is not controllable.' Does this mean I can't slim down and hope to stay slim the rest of my life?"

Forget it—I read the same article and it is absolutely untrue, as I have *proved* with over 10,000 ex-overweight patients, as well as in my personal case. Years ago I was 55 pounds overweight, had a severe heart attack, took off all that excess fat, and reduced to my ideal weight. I have stayed slim ever since. If I hadn't, I'm sure I wouldn't have stayed alive.

Don't let anybody discourage you. I assure you that you too can join my thousands of "formerly obese" and "formerly fat" teenagers who slimmed down and never became overweight again.

"Is it dangerous to skip a meal?"

Absolutely not; it's no tragedy to skip a meal, and don't let anyone tell you so. You may recall a case in recent years where a man and a young woman crashed in a small plane in the Yukon wilderness. They survived 42 days, skipping not just one meal but over a hundred meals! After they were rescued, it was found that neither one had suffered any lasting organic damage, even though they'd had nothing to eat or drink for 6 weeks except melted snow.

I don't recommend lengthy fasting or starvation diets for any teenager. I urge you not to reduce *below* your ideal weight, but to get to that ideal point and stay there for good looks and good health. But don't worry about skipping a meal; actually it's a very good idea when reducing.

"Are freakish, mystic diets safe and desirable?"

No—follow the advice of medical men on dieting and health care, not cultists, mystics, naturopathics, or any other unqualified faddist. Being "at peace with the cosmos," or following any other weird premise, won't cure you of serious diseases or cause you to lose weight. The Quick Teenage Diet, and my other speedy weight-loss diets, have been worked out carefully according to my experience in over fifty years of medical practice as an internist. These are not "fad" or freak diets—they have been *proved* effective and healthful by hundreds of thousands of ex-overweights. You can count on fewer calories, not more crackpot ideas, to reduce you.

"Are so-called 'health foods' preferable to others?"

The only special benefits in so-called "health foods" are the special profits produced for those who make and sell them. "Natural health foods" contain no special benefits. "Natural vitamins" have never been proved better than synthetic vitamins. There are no special merits in such faddist-promoted foods as blackstrap molasses, bone meal, wheat germ, or brewer's yeast. This has been proved conclusively.

"How can I tell if I'm a water retainer and should avoid salty foods and salt?"

A simple test is this: Press your finger for 30 seconds on the flesh at the mid-portion of your shinbone. When you remove your finger, if the indentation in the flesh remains for a while, you probably are a water retainer—and the depth of the hole indicates the extent to which this is true.

Try this test also over the outside or inside of the ankle, to see whether indentation remains after finger pressure is removed. If it does, check with your doctor, who will advise you accordingly about care and treatment. In case of any indentation at these spots, stop salting your foods or eating salty foods, ketchup, mustard, cocktail sauces, and so on.

Water retainers should drink *more* water, rather than less, on my rapid-reducing diets. The flow of fresh water helps to remove waste matter and to speed loss of pounds. However, if you are not following the Quick Teenage Diet exactly, the *extra* water won't help you.

"Are diets like the 'Diet Bread Diet' effective?"

The diet you refer to is advertised by a specific brand of "diet bread" and includes one or more slices of that brand of bread at every meal—of course. I have never known any people to lose weight as they wanted to, or as promised in the ads, on diets promoted by special interests and advertisers, such as this particular diet. Others include "must" eating of grapefruit, or consuming sugar as part of dieting (promoted by the sugar interests, naturally!).

Don't let yourself (or your family) be misled. No matter what advertising phrases may "seem" to mean, fat does not melt away fat. Without question, fat *adds* fat. This applies to highly promoted products such as safflower oil, corn oil, other vegetable oils, and any fats. Don't be fooled into thinking that any fats will help reduce you.

You must realize that the first aim of any of the commercial interests is to sell their product—and to try to concoct a diet requiring the use of the product. The primary purpose of creating an effective diet must be to slim you most quickly, surely, and healthfully—not to sell a specific product to the "overweight market."

"Do doctors approve of the dieting methods you recommend?"

My rapid-reducing methods have had enthusiastic approval from many doctors—but, as I suggest repeatedly, ask your own physician. From letters I have received, from comments by my readers, patients, and others in the past few years, I estimate that well over 1,000 ex-overweight doctors have reduced *themselves* and their families. Thousands more have instructed patients to "get

Dr. Stillman's book to get rid of your excess weight." That applies to overweight teenagers as well as adults.

"Are artificial sweeteners safe for teens?"

Government scientists are constantly checking artificial sweeteners, as noted by the ban on cyclamates (although no harm to humans has ever been traced to cyclamates, and many scientists say they are absolutely safe in the tiny amounts used in foods and drinks in the past). The sweeteners used today have been closely examined, and are constantly being reexamined—and will be banned if there is any doubt about their safety for humans. New artificial sweeteners are being developed also in an unceasing effort to improve taste and cut costs.

The artificial sweeteners in the foods and beverages in stores are certainly "safe" in normal use (of course, excessive use of anything, including "natural" salt, sugar, and other elements, can be harmful). Enjoy the benefits of "no-calorie" sodas and other artificially sweetened foods, and don't use worrying about them as an alibi to stuff yourself with high-calorie, sugary drinks and foods.

"I'm sure I stay fat and unattractive to spite my mother and father, so how can I possibly lose weight?"

I've heard this kind of amateur psychiatry from hundreds of patients, and I suggest, "Face it, that's just an excuse for not dieting. If you are *really* staying fat to spite your parents or a boyfriend or anybody else, then you may need help and should see a qualified psychologist or psychiatrist." Usually "psychological hatred or anxiety" is an empty alibi to permit self-indulgence.

I urge you to put aside blaming your deep, inner feelings about somebody else, and try the Quick Teenage

234

Diet for just one short week. When you lose 5, 10, or more pounds in that week, chances are that you'll be so thrilled that you'll stop blaming "spite" or other emotions, and go on dieting until you're slim and much happier. In my experience, most "angry," formerly fat, teenagers stop hating themselves and others when they finally see the desired mirror reflection of a slim, attractive figure.

> *"Dr. Stillman, how can I get over my doubts and discouragement over past dieting failures, and believe I can succeed with your methods?"*

Please reread the opening chapters of this book for the *facts* of my success in helping tens of thousands of overweights who had failed many times before on other diets. I think it is safe to say that no other diets in history have slimmed down so many ex-overweights as my swift weight-loss methods. A typical case history is in this letter from a young man not long out of his teens. I reprint it here not so much as a testimonial to the effectiveness of my reducing methods, but as an inspiration to you:

Dear Dr. Stillman,

I'm sure you must think it odd, receiving a letter from a total stranger like myself, but as I was sitting here reading your book for the 10th to 15th time, I came to the realization that I owe you a great deal of thanks for the help you've given me through your wonderful book.

I am 5′ 9″ in height, and in September of last year I weighed 220 pounds. I travel 9 months of the year in my work, and I'll be home in 2 weeks. When I get there, I think my family and friends are in for a shock. I now weigh 142 pounds, which I owe to your diet.

Looking back at my dieting and the 78 pounds I have lost, I wanted to just say "thanks" for helping people like me who have tried the drab, old-fashioned methods of dieting, which just don't work in many cases, as your book explains. I tried them all, with no results, but when I happened to see your book one evening I bought it, tried your diet, and I'm still amazed at the results I received.

Now when I look in the mirror, I like what I see; I enjoy going out in public; my whole life has changed. It was sure worth the effort, and when I get hungry for some high-calorie snack, I pick up your book and reread your text on the dangers of being overweight. It always does the trick, and I haven't gained back *one ounce*—and I don't think I ever will.

Let me say that with your diet, it's a two-way operation. You provided the method, and I provided the willpower. For a couple of total strangers, I think we make a pretty good team—and my waistline proves it.

Again, my thanks for your work and your book; I just hope that more people will take your advice and shed the extra fat before it's too late. I'm thankful I took it.

That letter tells the story of what your own happier future can be. You have the facts. You have the method that works, that has slimmed down thousands upon thousands of ex-overweights.

You have this book written specifically for you, the teenager. You can refer to it again and again for help and support. You can constantly refresh your knowledge of how to slim down swiftly at last—and how to keep slim for the rest of your life.

Our best wishes go with you—along with our congratulations upon reducing to the slim, trim figure you want.

14

Memo to Parents:
How to Help Your Teenager Slim Down and Keep Slim

This book is written to and for teenagers specifically. It is not intended for adults, nor for parents. However, since a great many teenagers say that their number-one overweight problem is *parents*, it makes sense that I add some words that may help you to help your teenager to slimming success. In my past medical practice, I have always discussed the reducing program with any parent accompanying a heavy teenager to my office.

The preceding chapters in this book tell your overweight teenager exactly how to slim down, using the methods that have proved successful with many thousands of young people through the years. In advising parents how they can be most helpful, I have found that the don'ts are almost as essential and effective as the do's. Since no one is more eager than you are to help your youngster, here are some necessary and useful guidepoints.

Honor your teenager's initiative and ability

When your overweight teenager goes on the Quick Teenage Diet (or other diet of his or her personal choice), it is his decision. It's not your move, even though you probably agree eagerly. In the teen years, your overweight youngster is capable of choosing an effective diet, and carrying through. Respect that independence, honor it, cooperate with it fully, without any nagging or niggling reservations.

One of the reasons why overweight teenagers slim down with exceptional success on the QTD is that they choose for themselves, and keep at it themselves. The dieting regulations are simple, as the youngster selects from a limited number of healthful protein foods.

Teens lose weight swiftly on this method of dieting, 5 or more pounds a week, week after week. That rapid weight loss is the "built-in will power," which helps them stay on the diet until they achieve their desired weight.

Please cooperate cheerfully in every way

Don't interfere. Don't offer your own advice (your teenager is guided by my experienced instructions).

Don't worry about your youngster's dieting, lest you communicate uncertainty and doubt. Your overweight teenager has been advised repeatedly in this book to have a medical checkup before going on any diet. See that this is done if he or she hasn't been checked by a physician for some time; no diet should be undertaken if there is some medical disorder, without the personal doctor's approval. Getting off the excess fat quickly is *good* for your youngster in every way, not bad—as some parents misinformed by old-fashioned prejudices may fear.

Keep in mind always that one of the best things that can happen to any overweight teenager is to slim down quickly. This usually leads to a generally happier outlook, including family relationships.

Your attitude as a parent can help make your youngster's dream of ideal weight come true. You can also encourage failure. It's a fact that many of my overweight teenagers have succeeded in reducing as they wished in spite of a negative parental attitude. But your wholehearted approval is desirable and can be a valuable boost toward ultimate success. A noted child specialist lists as essential to dieting success by overweight youngsters: "A planned program which seems reasonable to the youngster, and strong parental support and understanding."

Please read this book carefully

You can be more helpful to your teenage dieter if you will read every page of this book, not only the diets themselves. For instance, while the Quick Teenage Diet is the basic tool, your teenager is going to develop a totally new attitude toward food and eating.

Your thorough understanding and cooperation can help accomplish this. Unfortunately, it is not always easy for parents to offer their children less food. Frequently it means a drastic change in your own attitudes about food and health.

Put aside "fake fears"

A chubby, intelligent teenage girl told me hopelessly, "I can't diet successfully because my mother is sure that I'll drop dead if I don't eat enough. When I've had enough to eat at any meal, she pushes more food at me and insists, 'A little more won't hurt you, it's good for you—I don't want you to get sick.'"

The next time you find yourself saying anything like that, *stop!* If you don't believe me, at least honor the wisdom of Benjamin Franklin, who said, "I saw few die of hunger; of eating, a hundred thousand." Read the facts about "fake fears" in Chapter 13. You can't help being convinced that overeating is one of the greatest dangers to your teenager's health, today and for all the years ahead.

A national magazine investigating "The Shape of Americans to Come" reported, "There is a strong probability that the U.S. adult of tomorrow (your teenager) will not only be taller but also fatter. A study of the feeding patterns of 2,000 households in 12 states has indicated that *doting mothers are unknowingly sentencing their children to obesity and heart disease in later life by feeding them too much of the wrong kinds of food.*"

The report gives the reasons for this overfeeding: "Fearing that their children are not eating enough rather than too much, they stuff them . . ." Are you in this category, without realizing it? I've been amazed many times in my practice about how blind many parents are when they look at their own youngsters.

In a newspaper interview, the mother of a popular young singer admitted, "My daughter was a terrific eater. She had a lot of baby fat, and dieted from 180 pounds to 130 after she started singing. But I never noticed those things because I was so happy she was an eater."

Read the myth about "baby fat," as explained on earlier pages. Learn that from age 7 onward, children who are permitted (or, too often, urged) by their parents to become obese youngsters usually turn into obese teenagers and adults. *The longer they remain fat, the more difficult it becomes to change their eating habits.*

Help the optimistic spirit

In spite of their past failures, I have found that my overweight teenagers, once on the Quick Teenage Diet, are among the most optimistic individuals I have ever encountered. The great majority of them, boys and girls, are sure that this time they will not fail. That hope springs eternal in the human breast was never more true than with the chubby youngsters who see the numbers dropping on the scale after a few days on QTD eating.

Don't ever discourage your teenager about succeeding in reducing, even though you have seen him fail before. Remember, thousands of youngsters have succeeded on the Quick Teenage Diet after trying "everything else" with discouraging results. As long as the spirit is willing, the flesh will come off quicker with your encouragement. But if you sigh and seem pessimistic, the young dieter is more likely to give up.

Don't ever say "I told you so," or even indicate displeasure if your teenager falls off a diet. Don't criticize. Realize that the youngster is suffering enough because of the failure.

Don't scold. Instead, use the opportunity to encourage your teenager further, by saying, "Dr. Stillman says that you're not the first one to slip, nor will you be the last. He advises you to start right over again, more determined than ever to lose weight from now on." It's absolutely true; some of my most successful young dieters slipped off and started again, time after time before finally slimming down and staying slim from then on.

Don't worry about down-and-up weight loss and gain. Whatever excess fat is lost, even if only temporarily, is of some benefit. The idea is to strive not to slip and not to gain—but if weight does go up because of breaking the dieting rules, the next step is to take it right off again. The usual pattern of the down-and-up-and-down-and-up-and-down teenage dieter is that the "downs" soon outnumber the "ups"—and that's what counts in the long run.

If the 150-pounder goes down to 140, back up to 145, down to 135, up to 140, down to 130, up to 135, down to 125, up to 130, down finally to 120 pounds ideal weight in this instance (according to height and age), he or she is likely to stay about 120 from then on. The greatest encouragement is *seeing* that attractive, slim, trim figure —and *feeling* a wonderful new sense of buoyancy and gracefulness. The see-saw in weight is not at all unhealthy, as long as the trend is *down*. Again, encourage on the "downs," don't discourage on the "ups," knowing that the "downs" will win in the long run.

Don't give vent to your own exasperation by scolding or losing your temper. Realize that, whether it's apparent or not, overeating usually involves substituting food as an antidote to frustration, boredom, and unhappiness about being heavy. Your outspoken displeasure only increases the pressure to eat. Your understanding provides support and encouragement to succeed in slimming down. Most overweight youngsters have spent years learning the habit of overeating, and it's understandable that there can be some difficulty in unlearning it.

Don't nag . . . don't supervise too closely. This reducing program is something your overweight teenager is undertaking with personal volition and choice. A youngster when nagged tends to go on her (or his) "pest behavior" because she becomes upset, unhappy, unsure of herself, and often expresses her injured feelings by reacting antagonistically.

Cooperate, as your assistance is requested, but I urge you not to interfere or supervise. You know better than anyone that there's a big and crucial difference between assisting when wanted, as contrasted with taking charge when a teenager prefers to do "his own thing."

Essential Points to Help
Your Teenager Succeed

* *Take care not to upset your youngster while dieting* by asking too often how many pounds were lost each day. As weight goes down, the elated teenager is usually only too glad to volunteer this information. It's better that way.

* *Resist offering rewards* for dieting successfully. I know of a heavy boy whose wealthy father promised to give him a $1,000 Savings Bond for every 10 pounds of overweight he took off. The young man lost a few pounds, then quit dieting. Later he slimmed down on my Quick Teenage Diet, with no reward other than the wonderful boost of his own self-respect and the joy of having a slim figure.

* *Don't undertake any punishment* if your youngster fails. Instead, adopt the attitude that this is not a "failure" at all, but only a temporary setback. Encourage your overweight teenager to start all over again—and as many times as may be necessary. This builds character, and *success in slimming down eventually.* I know; I have seen this pattern so often through the years—two steps forward, one step back—but that youngster can't help but succeed finally. And the sense of triumph is all the sweeter for those who have fallen off a diet, more than once, perhaps, and ultimately "made it."

* *Try to maintain an unseeing eye toward any irritability* the youngster may show when dieting. Your teenager is doing something difficult and sometimes frustrating, in breaking ingrained eating patterns. Try to shrug off such personal irritations; don't snap or react angrily. As a parent, you can take it better than a youngster can. Your patience is a vital factor contributing to eventual success.

* *Don't ever show that you "feel sorry"* for your dieting teenager. Exhibit quiet understanding rather than unwanted sympathy. Your respectful attitude can work "miracles."

* *Avoid too much diet discussion—just give your overweight teenager the book, and let him or her take it from there.* This is very important, since the youngster will invariably respect the recommendations and instructions given in a book over those from a parent who is not an expert on the subject. In fact, while teenagers will take instructions from an authority, they generally *resist* the same advice from parents, often becoming stubborn and contrary and overeating out of spite.

* *Don't question the diet* because of inadequate knowledge or deep-seated prejudices. Don't ask, "Why no vegetables? Why no fruits? Why no good rich creamery butter—what's wrong with that? A piece of home-made cake, how could that hurt?" The Quick Teenage Diet, and all the diets in this book, provide more than adequate healthful eating for the growing teenager.

Again I urge you to *read the book*, absorb the facts of healthful, successful dieting that will remove any old-fashioned doubts and misconceptions you may hold. Success depends on avoiding unlisted foods; no matter how good certain foods may be in themselves—they just don't belong on this diet.

✻ *Realize once and for all that fat is unhealthy.* From age 7 upwards (many scientists include practically the entire life span), overweight becomes a health danger. Through the teen years and on through life, overweight tends to bring on higher blood pressure, diabetes, impairment of heart and other organs, an endless list of ills. And, shocking but true, a study of "super-fat" adults showed that *"more than half were grossly overweight before age 15."* The time to help your teenager slim down to ideal weight and better health for a lifetime is *right now*. Otherwise, there are likely to be increasingly serious health troubles ahead.

✻ *Be sure to read about the value of exercise and activity* in Chapter 10. You should gently encourage, but not push, your overweight youngster to increase his or her physical activity. This does not necessarily mean competitive team sports (which often don't provide enough sustained exertion). Exercise alone will never slim down an overweight teenager (or adult), but can be a vital aid in the reducing program. You can set an example by undertaking exercise and activity yourself, but *not* lecturing about it.

✻ *Be positive, not negative,* even if you are skeptical about your teenager's succeeding this time, because of past failures. A noted psychiatrist warns, "Many neurotic symptoms (among youngsters) are the result of negative parental attitudes. I have been impressed by how much

246

parental attitudes of trust or mistrust, confidence or doubt, determine youngsters' emotional response . . . Parental worry and insecurity can lead to anxiety in the youngster, parental blame to guilt and anger, parental doubt and dissatisfaction to emotional paralysis or obsessiveness."

* *Don't talk to others* about your teenager's dieting, without your youngster's consent. Don't ever discuss it with a stranger in your youngster's presence. Sometimes, if your teen is succeeding beautifully, you can tell another parent with a similar problem, but never when your child is around.

* *Provide a handy bathroom scale* so that your teenager on QTD (and from now on) can check his weight first thing every morning. If you are told what the day's weight is, you can supply applause if warranted, or encouragement.

The Importance of Setting an Example

Studies have shown that youngsters tend to be overweight usually—not always—if parents and others in the family are fat. If you are overweight, or both parents are overweight (not always the case), there's no question that you can help your heavy teenager by slimming down yourself. This is in line with the youthful attitude: "Don't tell me—show me!"

It helps, if you possibly can manage it, to run the household so that everyone is eating carefully, or at least the same foods in general as your overweight teenager on the Quick Teenage Diet. Certainly try to include in the family meals the essentials of QTD eating—lean meats, poultry, fish, and so on—along with the vegetables and side dishes others may demand. This fine protein eating is excellent for the health of all in the family.

Try not to put temptation before the young dieter at meals, or by filling the refrigerator or kitchen with no-no foods. This may be difficult in respect to other members of the family, but do the best you can. It's best not to display a creamy strawberry short cake, or to serve rich ice cream desserts, or other hard-to-resist high-calorie dishes.

Try to keep anyone in the family from snacking on high-calorie foods in front of the teenage dieter, at any time of the day or evening. It must be recognized that habit-breaking is rather difficult for most, so make every effort not to display extra temptations before the dieter's eyes. Here again you can set a good example by abstaining from those forbidden foods (check the QTD listing and instructions).

Make sure that you have the foods available for the Quick Teenage Diet (or whatever diet your youngster has selected). If you prepare the food, be sure to read the diet instructions—to cut all fat off meats, remove the skin from poultry, use no fats in cooking, and other essentials to quickest reducing.

Whether you make a competition of reducing at the same time as your overweight teenager depends greatly on the personal relationship. I believe strongly in family cooperation, but not in too much parental pressure, or imposing dieting restrictions if unwelcome. You'll have to judge how best to handle your own child in this respect. Some teenagers thrive on rivalry, while with others competition has a reverse reaction. Often the better course is for the parents to slim down without saying anything about it, except, if asked, to make some bland comment such as, "I decided I'd better take off some weight." Don't continually talk about it.

Start children with good eating habits

To keep from giving growing children at any age the bad habits of overeating and growing fat, I urge you not to overemphasize the importance of eating. Food should be served in a matter-of-fact manner, not as a reward or a reason for living. If children dawdle and show little interest in food, that's an excellent chance to train them to eat less; the child will naturally eat if he needs the sustenance.

If your child indulges in a "food jag," concentrating on one kind of low-calorie food, don't view it with alarm. This is common among youngsters; they soon get over it. Furthermore, one-dimensional eating for a while does no harm. Pediatricians as a whole agree that you shouldn't scold and yell at your kids for such eating eccentricities— they don't fall ill or starve because of the limited eating. If you make a big fuss, eccentric ways of eating and overeating may well become ingrained, instead of disappearing naturally. Remember, there's nothing wrong with a youngster that constant nagging won't make worse.

Don't force a child to eat. Don't threaten. Don't indulge in strange capers to encourage eating. Don't plead with the child, or hurry him. Don't bribe. Don't make him compete with other children in eating.

Don't brag about how much your child eats. Many become overweights by consuming big quantities as though it were an athletic triumph, or a sign of special prowess.

Start with small servings. If a very young child throws food on the floor, don't force the food on him—instead, remove the dish, and if the child is hungry, he'll eat later. A child can develop a permanent dislike for certain foods if you force them.

Don't be concerned if your child develops strong food preferences or prejudices—this is natural, and kids get over such flashes naturally if you don't make an issue of

it.

Keeping the weight down

Once your teenager has slimmed down, you can help him or her keep that weight down. Be guided by the instructions in Chapter 11 on Keep-Slim Eating so you know the best ways to keep your teenager slim.

Help your dieting teenager; don't hinder him. I have even known of foolish, over-protective parents who tried to sneak food to their heavy youngsters in reducing camps. One father sent his daughter a big box of candy wrapped in a bathrobe. No wonder that on visiting day at reducing camp, I saw one bulging youngster wearing a huge button stating, "Please Don't Feed Me."

Your Understanding Spurs Success

In your maturity and good judgment, you realize the truth of the adage, "No fathers or mothers think their children ugly." This understandable blindness tends to make parents overlook the physical, emotional, and psychological dangers of overweight for the heavy teenager. Your bulky teenager, whether outspoken about it or not, is likely inside to consider himself or herself "ugly." Your cooperation, as detailed here, can go a long way to help in the process of slimming down and being newly "beautiful."

Please don't think that I consider parents as ogres or guilty of all the problems of teenage overweight (I'm a parent myself!). You may be slim and setting a good example; yet your youngster may be heavy. Once a medical examination shows that there's no metabolic or other health disorder, my quick-reducing methods can accomplish wonders. Don't push—just let your teenager go by this book, and he or she will succeed in losing weight remarkably by giving that diet a fair chance, *just one short week.*

I don't think it's easy for you, but try to keep calm and

cooperative; don't lose your sense of humor. If your teenager abides by the Quick Teenage Diet faithfully, she will lose pounds and inches speedily, and go on losing down to slim, trim, ideal weight. No matter how little your youngster eats (or *seems* to eat, since "secret eating" may be a factor), if she is gaining weight, she is eating too much or not sticking to the diet. Your patience and understanding, providing the needed foods, following the cooking and serving guidelines, can be a vital ingredient in success.

You can be optimistic about your teenager's slimming success. As stated earlier, teenagers are aided in reducing by a generally faster metabolism than adults, by growth spurts until the late teens, by their natural eagerness and enthusiasm, and by the encouragement of losing weight quickly by my dieting methods.

Based on the success of so many others with these speedy, proved dieting methods, you too may be writing to me like many other happy parents (and happier ex-overweight teenagers), as in this letter: *"My teenage daughter has finally lost weight that she had been carrying for 5 or 6 years . . . and is losing still more."*

Happy, successful slimming to all of you!

INDEX

Acne, 26, 27
  anti-acne diet, 135–43
Alcohol, used in cooking, 189–90
Amino acids, 63
Anemia, iron deficiency, 227
Anti-Acne Clear Skin Diet, 135–43
Arterial disease, 26
Anorexia nervosa, 225

Baby fat, 17–18, 242
Beverages, 61–64
  recipes, 212–14
Bicycling, 154–55
Birth control pills, 222–23
Blood, 227
Blood pressure, high, 26, 57–58
Bouillon, 65
Boys. See Males.
Breakfast, necessity of, 12
Breathing. See Oxygen exercise.
Brillat-Savarin, Anthelme, 18
Broth, 65

Calcium, 55
Calisthenics, 155–59

Calories, 29
  daily intake
    exercise and, 39–40
    females, 37, 167
    males, 39, 167
  tables, 181–86
  used during exercise, 177
Candy, 74–75
Carbohydrates, in the body, 50–51
Chafing, 26, 27
Cheese. See Cottage cheese.
Chicken, 57
  recipes, 194–96
Cholesterol count, high, 73
Coffee, 138
Consommé, 65
Cottage cheese, 59–61
  recipes, 190, 207–09
Cowper, William, 97
Cyclamates, 234

Deep-breathing. See Oxygen exercise.
Dessert, 65
  recipes, 209–12
Diabetes, 26, 220, 246

Dividend Diet, 97–105

Edwards, Charles, 146
Eggs, 59
  recipes, 203–06
Exercise, 19–20, 23, 145–61
    (see also Oxygen exercise)
  bicycling, 154
  calisthenics, 155–58
  calories used during, 177
  daily calorie intake and,
    39–40
  isometric, 149–50
  isotonic, 149–50
  jogging, 152
  sports, 154–55
  swimming, 152–54
  walking, 150–52
Exercisers, mechanical, 158–59

Federal Communications
    Commission, 217
Females
  daily calorie intake, 37,
    166–67
  difficulty in reducing, 17
  ideal weight, 35–37
  menstruation, 28, 223
Fish, 57–59
  recipes, 197–203
Food and Drug Administra-
    tion, 63, 146
Franklin, Benjamin, 70, 241
Fruit, 70, 124–26
Fruit-Vegetable-Plus-Protein
    Diet, 124–31

Gelatin dessert, 65
  recipes, 209–12
Girls. See Females.
Gum, 73–74

Health foods, 232

Herbs, 66
High blood pressure, 26–27, 56
Hyperglycemia, 220
Hyperphagia, 220

Iron deficiency anemia, 227
Isometric exercise, 149–50
Isotonic exercise, 149

Jefferson, Thomas, 150
Jogging, 152
Johnson, Nicholas, 216

Keep-Slim Eating, 23, 46–7,
    163–81

Liquids-Only 1-Day Super-
    Quick Diet, 131–32
Males
  daily calorie intake, 39, 166–
    67
  ideal weight, 37–39
  puberty, 28–29
Meals
  number of, 75–76, 177
  skipping, 231
Meat, 55–57
  recipes, 189–97
Meat-Eater Super-Quick Diet,
    80–82
Mechanical exercisers, 158–59
Medical checkup, 14, 22–23
Menstruation, 28
  overweight and, 28
  weight gain during, 223
Mental illness, 225
Metabolism, 14, 164
  walking and, 150–51
Milk, 54–55
Mineral tablets, 61, 109, 175

253

Nervousness, 225

1-Day Super-Quick Diet, 131–32
Oxygen, 20
Oxygen exercise 20–21, 77, 105, 110, 147, 149–50
  isometric, 149–50
Physical examination, 14, 22–23
Polycythemia, 227
Posture, 148–49
Protein
  and cutting calories, 49–50
  S.D.A. (Specific Dynamic Action), 49–52
Puberty, 28–29
QTD Oxygen Exercise. *See* Oxygen Exercise.

Recipes, 187
Restaurants, eating in, 74

Salt, 137
Salt tablets, 159
S.D.A. (Specific Dynamic Action), 49–52
Seafood, 58–59
  recipes, 197–203
Seasonings, 66
Seborrhea, 26–27
Seven Day Diet, 85–95
Seven Day Dividend Diet, 97–105
Seven Day Quick Variety Diets, 111–24
Sex, overweight and, 224–25
Shellfish, 137
Sleep, 224
Skin, 26, 27

anti-acne diet, 135–43
care of, 140–42
Soda, 61–62
Soup, 65
Spices, 66
Sports, 154–55
Sugar, in the body, 50–51
Super-Quick Diets, 79–84, 131–32
Sweeteners, artificial, 234
Swimming, 153–54

Tea, 138
Turkey, 57

U.S. Federal Communications Commission, 217
U.S. Food and Drug Administration, 63, 146
Urea, 63
Uric acid, 63

Variety Diets, 111–24
Vegetable-Fruit-Plus-Protein Diet, 124–31
Vegetables, 70, 124–25
  calories in, 172–73
Vibrating machines, 158–59
Vitamins, 70–71
  natural vs. synthetic, 232
  tablets, 61, 109, 175

Walking, 19–20, 150–52
Waste elimination, 72–73, 230
Water, 62–64, 109–10, 175
  after exercise, 159
  loss of, 50, 51, 73–74
Wilde, Oscar, 169
Wine, used in cooking, 189–90

INVALUABLE REFERENCE BOOKS YOU WILL WANT TO OWN!

☐ **SEW SIMPLY, SEW RIGHT**
by Mini Rhea and Frances S. Leighton
Sew Simply, Sew Right is an easy-to-follow guide to making your own clothes, from the first stitch to the finishing touches which give your garment that professional look. (64-285, 75¢)

☐ **THE SINGLE GIRL'S GUIDE TO EUROPE**
by Andrea Kenis
How to handle money, manners, museums and *men*— and plan the best vacation of your life. (65-561, 95¢)

☐ **DON'T BANK ON IT!**
by Martin J. Meyer and Dr. Joseph M. McDaniel, Jr.
A step-by-step guide to making up to 13½% or more on your savings—all fully insured. (65-649, 95¢)

☐ **300 WAYS TO MOONLIGHT**
by Jerry LeBlanc
Three hundred ways to make money in your spare time— business ideas, things to make and sell, part-time jobs. There's something here for everyone! (64-274, 75¢)

BOOKS FOR GOOD HEALTH AND ENERGY!

☐ **GET YOUR SHAPE IN SHAPE**
by Fran Hair and Rita Chazen
Come alive—look more attractive in only 30 minutes a day with this new, effective exercise plan. (64-208, 75¢)

☐ **VIGOR FOR MEN OVER 30**
by Warren R. Guild, M.D., Stuart D. Cowan, and Samm Sinclair Baker
This book shows how to select certain enjoyable exercises and combine them with sensible eating procedures. It's packed with practical advice for dealing with the enervating pressures common to our competitive society, and sets up an ideal philosophy for safe, healthful, rewarding living. (64-139, 75¢)

JOIN THE MUSIC SCENE WITH
PAPERBACK LIBRARY!

☐ **JANIS JOPLIN:** *Her Life and Times*
by Deborah Landau

Deborah Landau has written an absorbing biography of Janis Joplin, the greatest white female blues singer of her generation. FULLY ILLUSTRATED (64-604, 75¢)

☐ **THE WORLD OF SOUL**
by Arnold Shaw

"Musicologist Arnold Shaw conducts his readers through Blues country, the black pop realm, Rhythm and Blues, Soul, Gospel and on down to James Brown, Otis Redding, and Aretha Franklin." (66-566, $1.25)
FULLY ILLUSTRATED —*Publishers' Weekly*

☐ **THE ROCK REVOLUTION**
by Arnold Shaw
This book traces the growth of rock music that was once thought of as a fad, now considered by many an art. FULLY ILLUSTRATED (65-487, 95¢)

☐ **COUNTRY MUSIC:** *White Man's Blues*
by John Grissim

This is no ordinary fan book. It is the inside, true account of the men and women who have made the Nashville sound into a million-dollar industry.
FULLY ILLUSTRATED (66-391, $1.25)